HIDDEN HISTORY *of* PEARSON FIELD

HIDDEN HISTORY *of* PEARSON FIELD

MARTIN MIDDLEWOOD

Foreword by Robert J. Cromwell, PhD

Published by The History Press
An imprint of Arcadia Publishing
Charleston, SC
www.historypress.com

Front cover: Walter Edwards ready to fly the first interstate mail, 1912. *Oregon Historical Society*.
Back cover: Silas Christofferson flies off Multnomah Hotel, 1912. *Oregon Historical Society*; *inset*: Evelyn Waldren, first Nebraska woman to fly, used Pearson Field. *Oregon Aviation Historical Society*.

First published 2025

Manufactured in the United States

ISBN 9781467158190

Library of Congress Control Number: 2025936200

Dedicated to all the men and women
who rose above Pearson Field
from its aviation beginning
and beyond.

CONTENTS

FOREWORD

I had the privilege of working for the National Park Service at Fort Vancouver National Historic Site for over two decades. The site has many intertwined and interdependent historic storylines that define the colonial history and development of the Pacific Northwest that we know today. These stories include the prehistoric Chinookan and Cowlitz Indians who used the resources and landscape from time immemorial that now make up the park site; the 1829–1860 British Hudson's Bay Company and the site of Fort Vancouver; the 1849–2012 U.S. Army Vancouver Barracks (the first U.S. Army post in the Pacific Northwest); and last, but certainly not least, the incredible aviation history associated with Pearson Field. All these stories are important and interdependent. The Hudson's Bay Company would not have set Fort Vancouver in this location without the presence of the Native Americans to trade with; the U.S. Army would not have established Vancouver Barracks in this location if it were not for the Hudson's Bay Company Fort Vancouver; and Pearson Field would not have been established if it had not been for the presence of the U.S. Army at Vancouver Barracks.

Through my role as the park's archaeologist, I became familiar with these many different storylines and historical events associated with Fort Vancouver but perhaps none as intimately as the stories associated with Pearson Field. I had both the privilege and challenge to be named the manager of Pearson Air Museum from 2013 to 2023. I remember a sense of trepidation when I was asked to take on this role, as my professional training was all in archaeology, an activity that forces one to look down toward and into the earth, not toward the sky, where aviation happens. I had never managed a museum before, much less an aviation museum, but I had the advantage of having worked with artifacts and collections and had even trained for a short while in artifact conservation. Most importantly, I had a passion for the history of aviation and in my youth yearned to be a naval aviator. The late discovery of my color blindness kept me from my teenage dreams, and aviation was not to be my career path.

Instead, with a background in academic and federal agency cultural resources management, I led the effort to rebuild Pearson Air Museum's collections and exhibits and had to dive deep into researching the many artifacts, people and stories associated with the site. It was during this time that I became associated with Martin Middlewood, who was a freelancer for *The Columbian* newspaper, researching and writing about historical figures who had lived in Vancouver and Clark County, bringing the stories of their lives to local readers. He made inquiries with me about several famous aviators and specific aviation stories related to Pearson Field, and I enjoyed sharing historical research with him. It was clear to me then that he had a passion for telling the stories of the past, a passion that shows throughout this volume. He brings these stories and these past aviators to life, allowing the reader to take a peek and a glimpse into the reaches of our past.

The story of Pearson Field is not just a story of one of the oldest continuously operating airfields in the nation, of over a century of aviation history related to one place. It is the story of dozens of people who made this history, who lived and worked and flew airplanes from this field. Much like the varied and interwoven histories associated with Fort Vancouver National Historic Site, the many stories and biographies presented in this volume weave together the history of Pearson Field. The many biographies of individuals who flew from Pearson Field, combined with the stories of individual aviation events that occurred at the field, create an entertaining, well-researched and lively history of Pearson Field as it has not been told before. It fills a needed niche in preserving this history and bringing the lives of some amazing personalities to a new audience, to preserve for future generations.

—Robert J. Cromwell, PhD

ACKNOWLEDGEMENTS

No published piece is a single person's effort. A book involves not just the writer but also many people assisting the author with research, editing, critiquing and guiding the book throughout its production and distribution before readers can, hopefully, hold it in their hands. This one is no exception. I want to thank the many organizations and people who helped me in various ways. The Clark County Historical Museum staff, especially Brad Richardson and Katie Bush, helped lead me to old news clippings and donated many of the photos in this book. Two Fort Vancouver Historic Site employees, Theresa Langford and Meagan Huff, helped immensely. Langford, cultural resources program manager, filled the hole left by Dr. Robert Cromwell, who left the NPS after twenty years. She answered my obscure questions while Huff, the curator, aided me in finding several photos for this book. The National Park Service also permitted a generous use of their photos. I wholeheartedly thank Mary Rose of The Friends of Fort Vancouver for her review of my manuscript, for standardizing Russian names, for the time spent talking with me about Pearson Field and for access to the Leverett Richards Collection photos. She also helped me find Russian photos. Robert Warren of the Oregon Historical Society helped me with several photos. For several years, the research staff at OHS generously helped me find resources, including oral histories of several women fliers in this book. I want to thank the Smithsonian National Air and Space Museum for using its photos the reader sees herein. No story about Clark County, Washington, would be complete without pictures from the long-running local newspaper, *The Columbian*. So, I must also thank Will

Cambell, publisher, for the generous use of photos from their archives. To Alan Mitchell, a Pearson Museum volunteer, a special thanks for reviewing my manuscript and the many emails exchanged about Pearson Field's history. Thanks also to the University of Alaska–Fairbanks for the photo of Vern Bookwalter; Proctor Enterprises, Wilsonville, Oregon, for the photo of Louis Proctor; Holly Chamberlain of the National Trust for the "flying flapjack" photo; and the Library of Congress for images too. For pulling files about Tex Rankin, Dorothy Hester, Danny Grecco and the Bohrers and donating several images for this book, I must not forget to thank the Oregon Aviation Historical Society. Thanks to John Shirron for donating the photo of Leah Hing's plane being returned. Finally, my deepest thanks go to Dr. Robert Cromwell, who for years generously responded to my many questions while he directed Pearson Air Museum and after he left for a new archaeologist position. He not only wrote the foreword to this book but also guided me through the gigabytes of research he'd obtained from the National Archives about the history of the airfield important to this book. While I had much help in pulling this book together, in the end, any mistakes, misinterpretations, errors or omissions are purely my responsibility.

PRELUDE

Open any history of flight book, and you won't find a mention of the oldest airfield in continuous operation, Pearson Field—today Pearson Airpark. Many of these publications are more about the aircraft than the people. Chroniclers of the broad history of flight leave Pearson Field out. For them, its history is hidden; the people who made the field a historic place disappear from such histories. This book is an attempt to place Pearson Airpark into the history of aviation because it had several firsts: the first U.S. letter delivered by dirigible in 1905, the first interstate airmail delivery, the first and second Soviet landings in the United States, the first wingless aircraft flight and others. It also attempts to highlight important personalities historians with broader perspectives consider trivial but have importance beyond Clark County and deserve wider consideration.

The land Pearson Airpark rests on today was once a trading center for Native Americans living in the area now designated Washington and Oregon. A mere seven miles west of the airfield, archaeological exploration during the early 1980s placed the original population in camps on the shore of Vancouver Lake six thousand years ago. The land's original peoples paddled the Columbia waterway to come together for trade. Until the Hudson's Bay Company came, we can assume the Indigenous presence in the area around Vancouver, Washington, was continuous.

Today a replica of Fort Vancouver stands exactly where the second fort was built in 1829. The airfield is east of the fort and is part of the Fort

Vancouver National Park. The fort established and run by the Hudson's Bay Company was a trading center. Indigenous peoples, trappers and HBC employees gathered pelts, primarily of beaver, and sent them to Europe, where they were made into felt hats. The fur company had control over a vast empire of Pacific Northwest land.

The Doctrine of Discovery facilitated conflicting claims on the Pacific Northwest. British and American claims overlapped with Spanish and Russian. In the end, Americans took the land from the Native Americans who lived in the Pacific Northwest. So, we must acknowledge the direct links back to those first peoples who occupied this area. Today, the area continues to thrive from trade, thanks to the Port of Vancouver.

In 1905, a mere two years after the Wright brothers made their first Kitty Hawk flight, eighteen-year-old Lincoln Beachey landed a dirigible from the 1905 Lewis and Clark Exposition in Portland, Oregon, at what would become Pearson Field. His descent marked the beginning of a historic and enduring relationship between the future Pearson Airpark and aviation, world-record endurance flights and aviation personalities.

Five years later, Charles Hamilton flew the first plane in the Willamette Valley. Amateur aviators appeared at the Vancouver Barracks polo field, Charles Watson and Silas Christofferson among the first. The polo field worked well for them because their self-fabricated planes needed little more than a smooth grassy area for takeoffs and landings. Since their flying was occasional, they pitched tents to work in, giving rise to an "airplane camp."

Even before an official airpark existed, the impromptu camp contributed significantly to the early growth of aviation in the Pacific Northwest. When the Army arrived, Pearson Field became a Pacific Northwest national airpower site. Beginning in 1921, aircraft were assigned there for forest patrol. The following year, the field was organized as the Vancouver Barracks Aerodrome, and it was christened Pearson Field in 1925. As a military airport between the two world wars, it played a significant role. During World War I, it provided the raw material—spruce—needed to manufacture aircraft. And as the Second World War raged, several pilots once based at the airpark turned to training pilots for the Army Air Corps, which would later transition into the Air Force.

Some may ask, "Why another book on Pearson Field?" First, it's three decades later, which provides us new information and perspective. Second, electronic research tools, online newspapers and new archives helped expand the story. Last, this book attempts a wider focus, pushing the story of Pearson Field into the mainstream of aviation history by taking the stories of the personalities who made Pearson Field important and who went on to make significant contributions to American aviation history—because of their experiences at Pearson Field. Like Jon Walker's excellent *A Century Airborne: Air Trails of Pearson Airpark*, this one roughly follows a chronological order. Unlike it, however, readers can crack this one open to any section sparking their interest and still broadly follow the story of Pearson Field.

Despite three books on Pearson Field, there remains much more about the airpark to be explored and written about: Its legal struggles to exist; the misunderstanding between The Historic Trust and the National Park Service; the role of the Pearson Historical Society in successfully establishing Pearson Museum; the details of the Vancouver City Council and the Commercial Club (later the Chamber of Commerce) in establishing the municipal airfield; and the entire 321st Squadron story, which is only touched on here. All these and others are left to a future local historian to research and explain.

I
APPROACHING CLOUD LAND

Introduction

Once the heavens were the place for gods, not men. In the Bible, Ezekiel 1 describes cherubim with four wings and the Ark of the Covenant depicts cherubim and seraphim with wings. Daedalus and Icarus soared through the air on wings of wax and feathers in Greek mythology. Excited by his flight, Icarus flew too close to the sun, melting his wings and falling to his death in the sea. The myth is a foreshadowing of human desire for flight and its cost.

In aviation's early days, failure trumped success. Devices of all kinds were proposed. Most never worked. Inventors have imagined human-powered flight since Leonardo da Vinci in the Italian Renaissance. Da Vinci studied the flight of bats, birds and kites. From these studies, he drew various flying machines, including the ornithopter, a machine mimicking a bird's flight, as well as corkscrewing helicopters, human-powered gliders, even parachutes. Then, in the 1700s, lighter-than-air craft, hot-air balloons were the first to leave the ground, but their "pilots" lacked control and drifted at the wind's whim.

Da Vinci's aeronautical works weren't published until the late 1800s, leaving more than a century gap between serious flight work until wealthy industrialist Dr. Otto Lilienthal (1848–1896) made several successful full-sized glider flights between 1891 and 1896. Lilienthal even created a symmetrical domed hill nearly fifty feet high to catch the wind from any

Otto Lilienthal flying his Lilienthal 1894-19 Gliding Sailing Apparatus with his legs swung to the left for control. *National Air and Space Museum.*

direction. Because his flights were repeated and well-documented, many credit him as the first person to fly. Newspapers and magazines published photos of him in midair, which excited the public and science about heavier-than-air flight becoming a reality. His work originated the concept of the modern wing. Unfortunately, he died before that was recognized.

It wasn't until 1977 that the first sustained pedal power lifted the Gossamer Condor above the earth, making Lilienthal's dream of human-powered flight real. The ninety-six-foot wingspan of Gossamer Condor, a lightweight plane using pedal power to turn a propellor, lifted off the ground for one mile. The Gossamer Albatross made the second human-powered flight two years later. The pilot pedaled the plane twenty-three miles to cross the English Channel, only to collapse at the end of his flight. For now, it seems dreams of human-powered aircraft remain doubtful. Nevertheless, we cannot rule out the advances of sophisticated technology.

Certainly, the Wright brothers' December 1903 flight caught the twentieth-century imagination and led to innovating heavier-than-air flight, making the world reconsider soaring the sky. But the brothers built on the work of Lilienthal, adopting his aerodynamic data as a starting point in their own research. As important as the brothers are to aviation innovation, every floating or propelled airship needed a place to land. Originally a polo ground for the Army, Pearson Field commenced its aviation history when a dirigible piloted by an eighteen-year-old landed on the Vancouver Barracks polo field two years after the Wright brothers' flight.

Within a few years, novice aviators had set up an aviation encampment there, making the place a hub of aviation innovation and experimentation. If they were anything, they were primarily mechanics. These enthusiasts knew some basic concepts of lift and drag and little more. However, lack of knowledge didn't curb their desire to fly. They designed their own aircraft from scratch, from a kit or by modifying a purchased plane.

The history of Pearson Airpark fits neatly between Otto Lilienthal's human-powered glider flights and Chuck Yeager's breaking the sound barrier in 1947. In 2025, Fort Vancouver celebrated its two hundredth anniversary. What's remarkable is that same year, Pearson Airpark marked one hundred years since it was dedicated as a military field, although civilian pilots were flying from there as early as 1910. Following the early experimenters of aviation, many early twentieth-century innovators, enthusiasts and daredevils carried on the long tradition of aviation firsts on the north bank of the Columbia River at a place called Pearson Field, reputedly the oldest aviation field in the United States, certainly the oldest in continuous use on the West Coast.

Balloonists

Like the world, Clark County's first exposure to flight came in the form of lighter-than-air balloons. While Pearson Field's polo field never saw a hot-air balloon, the city around it did. By the time Vancouver first saw ballooning, balloons had been flying for more than one hundred years. One crossed the English Channel in 1785. The first manned balloon flight in America occurred in 1793. Balloons filled with hot air were safe enough. But all lighter-than-air craft were lifted by gas, often by explosive hydrogen. A balloon crash over Ireland in 1785 burned one hundred houses in Tullamore town.

Ten years after the first balloon flight, George Washington observed a Frenchman, who had crossed the English Channel in a balloon, lift off from a Philadelphia, Pennsylvania prison yard in a hydrogen-filled craft. After ascending nearly 5,800 feet, he landed in Gloucester County, New Jersey.

During the Civil War, the Union and Confederate armies used balloons to see behind enemy lines and direct cannon fire at the enemy. These lighter-than-air craft reached one thousand feet and offered a bird's-eye view of all beneath them.

At least three balloonists—not counting the 1905 Lewis and Clark Exposition dirigible flights—raised aloft from different places in Clark County, including, in the early 1920s, a balloonist who went aloft from Esther Short Park. The first lighter-than-air craft floating in the Clark County sky weren't the eighteen-year-old Lincoln Beachey's two flights from Portland's 1905 Lewis and Clark Exposition. At least two balloonists beat him into the atmosphere—although with much less control and finesse.

In April 1890, Vancouver's first balloon ascent took Professor William Lang skyward. He floated up from Thirteenth Street, reaching five or six hundred feet as a crowd of locals craned their necks to keep him in view. Local papers dubbed this modest ascension a success. They did not mention the professorial descent, so we may assume it was without problems.

The following year, Professor Vilas lofted a balloon from the corner of Twelfth and Main Streets. The professor's hot-air balloon lifted beyond Lang's height, reaching eight hundred feet as about 1,500 Vancouverites watched. When his balloon reached eight hundred feet, he bailed out. The onlookers must have gasped as the professor plunged earthward, seemingly to his death. Instead, Vilas had just made the first parachute jump in Clark County. His parachute silks unfurled, and he drifted to the ground beneath an enormous white parasol. However, on landing, Valis narrowly skirted a white picket fence, preventing the county's first jump from ending in disaster. Nothing is said about how or where the balloon came down.

As Pearson Airfield was revived after World War I, continuing through the 1920s, balloonists gathered crowds at Esther Short Park and the county fair. *Clark County Historical Museum.*

A 1911 issue of *The Vancouver Columbian* recalled that "some years back" a Dick Miller launched his balloon on July 4, 1907. Miller evidently lacked both the professional skills of a Lang and the foresight of a Vilas, who dropped to earth under silk. Instead, Miller and his balloon descended not to dry land but into the wet Columbia River and had to be rescued.

At the mercy of the wind, balloons could control only their altitude. However, airships filled with hydrogen appeared around 1900 and were propelled like the dirigible Beachey piloted. These new dirigibles had an engine spinning a propeller, which allowed a pilot to control the direction and speed of the craft. Often several hundred feet long, they traveled hundreds of miles. Such airships became the first passenger airliners and later weaponized military aircraft.

First U.S. Airmail Letter: Lincoln Beachey (1877–1915)

Captain Thomas Baldwin needed a pilot for his airship that would be part of the 1905 Lewis and Clark Exhibition in Portland, Oregon. The skills he sought were no fear of heights and mechanical proficiency. Piloting the dirigible, his employee had to traverse a narrow scaffolding under the inflatable without fear. Back on the ground, he'd keep the high-performance Curtiss motors operating. The captain found a suitable eighteen-year-old.

Young Lincoln Beachey flew Baldwin's airship from the 1905 Lewis and Clark Exposition in Portland, visiting Vancouver twice during the exposition. On August 3, he made the first controlled flight across the Columbia River to Washington State, piloting the *City of Portland*, which was later renamed for its sponsor, the Knox Gelatine Company.

On his more memorable second voyage, Beachey carried the first packet of airmail messages in U.S. history, just two years after the Wright brothers' first flight. Unaware, the U.S. Post Office never sanctioned the delivery. Any concerns about airmail were still years away. Lifting off the exposition fairgrounds on September 19, 1905, the sky boy flew his second trip over the Columbia River, setting the bulbous ship down on the barracks parade ground as awed Vancouver residents watched. The teenager reached inside his jacket and handed several letters to Win Carson, the postal clerk, who lugged the mail to the Fourth and Washington Streets post office in Vancouver. Beachey also carried a message addressed to General Constant

Williams, commander of the Department of the Columbia, from Theodore Hardee, assistant to the exposition president.

Hardee's message conveyed the president's compliments to the general and expressed "the hope that this uniquely transmitted message will be delivered to you promptly and safely." He flattered the commander by offering "the distinction of being the first to have ever received [such] a document." Closing self-congratulatorily, Hardee finished, "And President Goode and myself will share your honors in being the first to transmit the same."

Returning, the boy skipper hit a harsh northeast wind that drove the blimp in the wrong direction. Beachey floated over Clark County for almost two hours, shattering the previous duration record by twenty minutes before landing in A.B. Gilmore's farm near Orchards. After a struggle to lash the ship down, it was deflated and carted back to Portland on a farm wagon, along with a tired aeronaut. According to Bob Cromwell, former Pearson Air Museum manager, there are no records of Williams returning a message with Beachey. If one existed, it went humbly back to the exposition in the same wagon with Beachey and the *Gelatine*.

After Beachey's flight, photo postcards appeared. One of the airship, *Gelatine*, carried this note: "Vancouver, Wash. April 15, 1906; In the Good Old Summer Time [*sic*] a letter to you by to-morrows mail. Very Truly yours, Win." The signer was probably the Vancouver postal clerk, Wingenald "Win" Carson, who received the first batch of airmail letters ever sent eight months earlier—and had them delivered by the city's postal carriers.

During the exposition, the young pilot flew twenty-three flights. Later he emerged as America's first aerobatic pilot, flying upside down and in loop-the-loops. Beachey became known as the "California Flying Fool," and others imitated him. As aviators' deaths piled up, the press blamed Beachey for the fools who followed him.

After the death of Charles Walsh (the first to fly Vancouver skies), Beachey gave a speech at the San Francisco's Olympic Club. From behind the lectern, he gazed at the audience, saying, "Gentlemen…I'm through with flying." He went on to say that death had always been his opponent, noting how Walsh's wife begged her husband to cut spirals from his demonstrations and how a few days before it was a reverse spiral that killed him. Beachey continued, saying he'd seen Mrs. Walsh and her two babies passing through a train station, making him feel as if he'd murdered Walsh. He ended that unless the U.S. military asked him to fly in a war, he'd was done. The audience sat with mouths agape in disbelief.

A stereoscopic image of Lincoln Beachey leaving Portland in the *Gelatine* delivering an unofficial "airmail" letter to General Constant Williams, Vancouver Barracks commander. *Library of Congress.*

Soon after, a vaudeville company offered Beachey $1,000 a week just to stand on the stage with his airplane and speak about aviation, and he accepted. Then he heard Adolphe Pégoud flew a loop in France, and he decided he'd try the same in Hammondsport, New York. He tried and failed, crashing and clipping two bystanders, killing one and critically injuring the other. Curtiss built a plane that might withstand the loop and convinced Beachey to try again. He did and successfully made the loop.

In 1915, Beachey died in an accident. When his new monoplane crumbled under him, unable to take the stress of his dive, he lost control and plowed into San Francisco Bay. When found, the drowned pilot had his hand on the fuel petcock. He'd shut off the fuel line, thinking he'd prevent a fire. News flashed around the world of America's most famous flier's death. A nation was in mourning. So many calls came through San Francisco switchboards that the telephone system was jammed for twenty-four hours. Theaters carried newsreels of the fatal flight. Boys who had viewed his flights showed their sadness over their hero's death by wearing black armbands. San Francisco Mayor James Rolph spoke at Beachey's funeral. The procession led by the police was blocks long. At the cemetery, a rifle volley was fired and taps played, sending the soul of America's first famous flier skyward.

POLO FIELD TO AIRFIELD

What do Clark County historians mean when they mention the polo field at the Vancouver Barracks? Where exactly was that field? It's a little confusing, because it turns out there were at least three different polo field sites.

In 1849, the Mounted Rifles arrived at the Hudson's Bay Company's Fort Vancouver to begin the fort's transition to the United States. The area southeast of the fort along the Columbia River was called Jolie Prairie, or in English, "pretty prairie." Soon after the HBC left for Canada in 1860, the fort burned to the ground. Eventually, the area was rebuilt and became the Vancouver Barracks. From the late 1800s into the 1930s, soldiers played polo in several places around the grassy areas where the old fort once stood.

Polo, one of the oldest known team sports, likely started as early as the fifth century in Persia, today's Iran. The modern polo field is 300 yards long by 160 yards wide or about 10 acres—the size of 9 football fields. Pearson Airpark today is 134.4 acres and could easily hold 13 polo fields. So, where were the original ones?

Following the Europeans, the U.S. Army used polo to train its cavalry officers, first at Fort Riley, Kansas, in 1896. West Point adopted the game in 1901. The Army believed polo taught physical fitness, teamwork, riding skills and mounted combat. Instead of sabers and lances, the riders used mallets, or sticks, to strike a three-and-a-half-inch ball while charging down the three-hundred-yard field in less than a minute, a speed as fast as a cavalry charge.

Local history buffs know that nineteenth-century polo players used the parade ground for the game. However, two maps published by the Vancouver Barracks, one from 1912 and another from 1928, show two different but official polo fields. That leaves a mysterious gap between the parade ground's use and the first map.

The local newspaper started running occasional articles mentioning the polo field and its games about 1909. But casual polo games may have been held earlier on impromptu fields. A March 1899 edition of the *Vancouver Weekly Columbian* published a brief about an officer's polo injury but didn't mention the polo field location. According to a National Park Service report, "Riptide on the Columbia," by Donna Sinclair, officers participated in polo matches on the parade ground throughout the later nineteenth century.

Often the parade ground and the polo grounds are confused and blended into one large grassy field. There was an unofficial polo field on the parade ground and at least two official polo fields at Vancouver Barracks. The field's placement on the parade ground is unknown, as are the number of games played. In 1905, Lincoln Beachey landed the airship *Gelatine* at the Vancouver Barracks parade ground near the Howard House, which is often said to be the polo grounds. This further confuses the location of the polo fields.

Not far from Beachey's landing spot, the first impromptu airfield was built around 1910 and was in the grassy area just west of today's Pearson Air Museum, between the museum and the reconstructed Fort Vancouver. At

Four mounted polo players, possibly military personnel. The Vancouver Barracks held polo games in the late nineteenth century until the Great Depression. *Clark County Historical Museum.*

this time, pioneer aviators Silas Christofferson, Walter Edwards and Charles Walsh erected tents and began using the flat polo area to build, repair and fly their airplanes. About the same time, the "aviation camp" started up.

By 1911, the camp was bustling. The Vancouver Commercial Club saw an opportunity to promote the city by hosting an aviation show there. Their idea fell through, and the club had to wait nearly two decades to boost local aviation's commercial viability.

The Army still used mounts, and intermingling airplanes with mules became a problem at the polo grounds. Second Field Artillery mules seemed to like airplanes and those under construction at the field particularly. The four-legged beasts sometimes swarmed around the planes. Even alone, the mules caused trouble, often going on walkabouts solo, frightening schoolchildren, cows, calves and colts. Army mules even left the barracks grounds, breaking down fences and causing runaways.

Aviators and mules confronted each other in 1911. Colonel George K. McGunnegle, Vancouver Barracks commanding officer, denied aviators permission to fly from the drill field to protect the Army mules' daily run. He feared the takeoffs and landings would stampede the animals. Silas Christofferson argued that flying before the mules had their morning exercise wouldn't bother them. The major agreed and granted his request.

A year later, several locals sent letters to Major Edward F. McGlachlin, commander of the Second Artillery at the barracks. The Ellsworth Mother's Club protested, claiming the mules nearly obliterated a footpath for children walking to school.

During World War I, the barracks shifted its attention to war. The construction of the Spruce Production Division's Cut-Up Plant in 1918 covered the polo field, ending polo playing until after the war. All flights, except for the Forest Patrol fire searches—a joint effort between the U.S. Forest Service and the emerging Air Service—ceased.

Polo playing didn't reboot at the barracks until 1924, when Lieutenant Frank Strickland and other polo enthusiasts reestablished the sport at the barracks. In the late spring of 1924, the Northwest International Polo Tournament was held there. From May 9 to May 18, 210 ponies took part in the tournament at the Vancouver Barracks polo grounds. Competing teams from Camp Lewis; Vancouver, British Columbia; and Oregon Agricultural College were vigorously committing their practices to wresting away the trophy won by the barracks the previous year. The sheltered grandstand seats held one thousand people overlooking the field, protecting the audience from the occasionally wet skies.

There were six teams participating in the tournament, and the commander of the Third Division, General Babbitt, was among the visitors. During the ten-day event, the games were broadcasted not by radio but by "aerial advertising," according to an April 26 *Columbian* story. Colonel Jason M. Walling and Lieutenant Oakley Kelly flew across Washington, Oregon and Idaho, dropping five thousand handbills printed by the *Vancouver Evening Columbian* over "each town and city in the northwest that the aviators visited."

At that time, polo also entertained city residents. In 1928, a second field appeared on a Vancouver Barracks map. It shows the game field's location west of Fort Vancouver at a site archaeology has revealed as HBC's Kanaka Village. This field was laid out during polo's golden age in Vancouver, 1925 to 1931. A grandstand holding five hundred spectators was started in 1926, and polo games were played on Sundays and covered by *The Columbian*. That season, the barracks team beat the Portland Hunt Club 6–2, with Captain T.A. Harris scoring twice. Although competitors' spouses and others paid for box seats, the number of seats attests to the game's local popularity.

Competitions held on the barracks grounds attracted large crowds of local spectators who came to see tested polo players and officers compete mounted atop horses with names like Brownie, Polly and Winkles. Sweet Patootie, a favorite mount of Captain T.A. Harris, was sold in May 1928, as reported in *The Columbian*. The horse was known throughout the Northwest but should be retired to a saddle horse and not play polo again, said the newspaper's editorial.

Spectators also visited the Vancouver Barracks grounds to attend polo games and other events, such as Army air circuses featuring stunt flying. In September 1927, four of fourteen days of polo included stunt flying by army pilots. Lieutenant Oakley Kelly and his aviators performed "all sorts of spectacular air stunts," said *The Columbian*.

By 1936, the oval polo fields had disappeared from barracks maps. They were replaced by barracks for the Civilian Conservation Corps (CCC), established in 1933. The new CCC barracks were constructed on the western side of the barracks property in 1936, where the polo grounds had previously been located.

Starting with the first flight across the Columbia River in 1905, the Vancouver Barracks polo field became an aviation camp for pilots, wannabe pilots, engine mechanics and aviation groupies. Sometime around 1911, the polo grounds attracted multiple young fliers who set up an aviation camp where they built, repaired and attempted to fly airplanes—sometimes to the consternation of the local citizens. The first flight over Vancouver stampeded army mules and sent a frightened mother and her children skedaddling.

Polo died out in Clark County in the early years of the Great Depression. When Lieutenant Oakley Kelly arrived as commander, his pilots shared the field with polo players. He even helped promote the 1927 tournament. It took another two decades before the army abandoned horses in war. It wasn't until March 1942 that the U.S. Army deactivated the mounted cavalry. Today, references to the "polo field" suggest the entire grassy green area between the Columbia River and the Vancouver Barracks and include the parade ground and Pearson Airfield.

Because the former flying field's name has changed several times, what to call it can be confusing. Established in 1921 by the U.S. Army, it was called the Vancouver Barracks Aerodrome. In May 1925, J.L. Hines, the secretary of war, gave Lieutenant Kelly permission to rename the field after Lieutenant Alexander Pearson Jr., who died the year before in a crash preparing for his second Pulitzer Race. The field was dedicated that year with a massive celebration. Flying at the field was mostly inactive during the year and a half the Spruce Cut-Up Plant operated during World War I, except for reconnoitering flights for forest fires. The military portion of the field went inactive again during World War II. The Army transferred it to the City of Vancouver for civilian use in 1946 and kept the name Pearson Airfield, a name that today refers to both airfields.

2

BREAKING THROUGH THE CLOUDS

Flies off Hotel: Silas Christofferson (1890–1916)

Obsessed with internal combustion engines, the Iowa-born Silas Christofferson edged them to rev as fast as they'd run. When he was six, his parents moved to California, where later he learned to fly. In 1910, he moved to Portland to work as an auto mechanic for Fred A. Bennett. According to Salem's *Statesman Journal*, Bennett and Silas formed the Bennett-Christofferson Airship Company there, with $3,000 of capital stock. Bennett's wife, Mary, was also a stockholder.

Christofferson put his knowledge of mechanics to the test, making engines for the cars, boats and airplanes he built whine loudly. He established a local reputation as a race-car driver by winning the Rose Festival race in 1910 and 1911. He also won the Pacific coast motorboat championship in 1911 racing in the twenty-five-foot boat class. Funded by Bennett, Silas and his brother Harry built a Blériot-like monoplane. However, when tested, the plane didn't do well because the brothers hadn't obtained exact specifications. Disappointed, Silas returned to California and took flying lessons in a Curtiss biplane.

Inspired by Lincoln Beachey, who dirigibled across the Columbia River, Christofferson pushed the limits of his airplanes, regularly endangering his life. Early planes were fragile homemade affairs cobbled together with wings;

small, noisy engines; and faith. While flying a home-built contraption spelled daring, the genuinely heroic performed stunts to press their skill, reap public attention and attract benefactors.

In his early flying days in Vancouver, Christofferson desired a bit more solitude during his 1911 Blériot tests. He relocated from the polo grounds to Lowell Hidden's pasture. After a few mishaps, Hidden grew concerned for his barn. The gasoline engine was likely to spark a grass fire. So, he informed the young flier that if he wanted to continue using the pasture, he needed to obtain some protection for the barn. The outcome was a lease with payments big enough to cover the barn.

To hold public attention, Christofferson's stunts grew more daring. He broke balloons floating his wingtip eighteen inches above the ground to show his skill. Any minor miscalculation—or microburst—and his wing could bite the dirt, flipping him to the ground. Early pilots broke bones as often as rodeo riders.

Silas flew Clark County's first women through the Vancouver skies in 1912. One of them, Edna Becker, divorced her husband and married the young aviator. At her new husband's shop in California, Edna helped build airplanes and after his death earned her pilot's license.

While Christofferson was doing a series of exhibitions in Southern Oregon, a schooner capsized on the Coos Bay bar. He flew a *Coos Bay Times* reporter over the bar, producing what may have been the first aerial news story. Although Christofferson's flight over the capsized ship couldn't save the crew, he gained the admiration of the community through the drama of the event.

During the June 1912 Rose Festival, Christofferson delivered on his promise to fly off the newly opened Multnomah Hotel (now Embassy Suites) in the heart of downtown Portland at 319 SW Pine Street. At first, Phillip Guverutz, president of the Multnomah Hotel Company, intended to make his first airplane flight off the hotel he owned with Christofferson. He decided wisely that probably wasn't the best first flight for anyone. The Curtiss Pusher craft Christofferson flew was hardly sturdier than a kite. To spin the behind-the-wing propellers, the daring pilot purchased one of Glenn Curtiss's first OX-5 V-8 engines to boost the horsepower needed for the stunt. Helpers hustled to fit the hotel roof with a 175-foot plank runway 30 feet wide. The biplane, weighing 850 pounds, was disassembled and rebuilt on the hotel roof for the event with Danny Grecco's help.

When asked why he would take such a risk, Christofferson answered he wasn't going to copy other stunts; he wanted to be original, adding this would be the first exhibition of its kind. Adolf Behrend, a German flier in Portland at the time, discouraged the risky flight, saying any pilot making such risks would forfeit his life eventually.

Fifty thousand onlookers gathered on Portland streets and rooftops to watch. There's even a photo of a film crew recording the event, but the film itself is lost. Christofferson's nervous but supportive wife, Edna, stood by watching. Her husband's plane rolled over the clanking wooden planks, and she released an audible sigh when he lifted off the hotel roof into the air. Once he was in the air, she knew her husband was safe.

Leaving the wooden runway and his wife on the hotel roof, Christofferson headed north toward the Columbia River, first crossing over the Willamette River before landing at the aviation camp at the polo field twelve minutes later. Besides being the first airplane flight ever off the roof of a building, his flight from Portland was also the first interstate airplane flight between Oregon and Washington, as well as the first heavier-than-air flight across the Columbia River. In an airplane that was little more than a kite with an engine, his daredevil risk made him famous, launching him into the first rank of aviators.

Early birdman Silas Christofferson launches his lightweight plane from the top of the multistory Multnomah Hotel in Portland, Oregon, during the June 1912 Rose Festival. *Oregon Historical Society*.

The next day, the *Morning Oregonian* praised the twenty-four-year-old's daring, saying, "It remained for the unlicensed ex-automobile racer to be the pioneer in trusting his heavier-than-air machine in a start from the midst of the business center of a great city." Perhaps the critical German aviator was mistaken about Silas.

Soon after, he moved to San Francisco and with his wife began building planes and instructing pilots. Some of these were "float planes," which later evolved into seaplanes. On the exhibition circuit, he charged five dollars for an aerial junket. Young Christofferson set a new American altitude record of almost sixteen thousand feet by flying over Mount Whitney in just fifty-six minutes.

Two years later, Christofferson was back in Portland, flying with an aerial movie photographer. During the flight, he bent down to fix his toe strap. "Just as I bent over a great gust of wind swept under one of my tilting planes and the body control bars…pulled over to one side.… One caught me squarely in the middle of the back." Soon the machine was "standing on its ear." The cameraman reached over and pulled the controls back so his pilot could take command again. His quick action averted an accident.

On Halloween 1916, Christofferson died in California while test-flying a prototype, trying to prove the aircraft was the "safest ever made." A cheering crowd watched him take the biplane through maneuvers. Then, about two hundred feet (some accounts say one hundred) above the earth something went wrong, releasing the pilot from the sky and sending him earthbound as his wife watched in terror. Edna was among the first to reach her husband, and she directed men, including the pilot's brothers, to get Christofferson into an ambulance. The driver hurried her twenty-six-year-old husband's broken body to a nearby hospital, where he died. Edna buried him next to Lincoln Beachey, who died by crashing into San Francisco Bay a year earlier.

It's notable that Silas had five brothers, three of whom also contributed to aviation: Goodsell, Harvey and Harry. Goodsell died in a crash when a student froze at the controls and plowed into the ground. Harvey, piloting his plane cross-country, went into a tailspin and crashed. Brother Harry avoided an aerial death and lived until 1968.

First over Vancouver: Charles Walsh (1877–1912)

About 1907, Charles "Fred" Walsh filed for bankruptcy after investing in gold at Goldfield, Nevada, which rendered him a financially devastating loss. He'd previously worked as a railroad engineer and for an oil refinery. His insolvency forced him to move his wife and daughter back into his father's home.

While working as an elevator operator, he started learning about aircraft and drawing designs. Walsh assembled a group of financiers in 1909 to launch the San Diego Aeroplane Manufacturing Company, California's first aircraft manufacturer. He was a vice president and general manager. At that time, the company reputedly built the largest airplane of the day out of spruce and piano wire. It had 7-foot-long propellers, a wingspan of 50 feet and a body 140 feet long, almost the length of three ranch-style homes today.

In 1911, Walsh tried for his pilot's license and failed. He not only failed but also crashed and fell 100 feet without injury. Flying before the Aero Club of California, he'd completed half his circuit when a control wire broke, sending him earthward. Had he passed the exam, he would have become the only licensed pilot west of the Mississippi River.

During the early days of aviation, the only moneymaking route for pilots was risking their lives flying daredevil stunts in shows for part of the gate receipts and hopefully to attract patrons. Risky maneuvers brought in larger audiences and a bigger gate. Someone from the Pacific Aviation Company based in Portland asked Walsh if he wanted to fly for money in their upcoming West Coast shows. He'd fly with the H.W. Manning group under the banner of the Pacific Aviation Company, which had set up a camp on the Vancouver Barracks polo field. Silas Christofferson's brother Harry worked for the same group as a mechanic, and Walsh hired him.

In May 1911, Portland audiences saw Walsh fly four times daily in exhibitions. The crowd gasped during fast takeoffs, one-thousand-foot climbs and severe banking. He also gave the city's notables their maiden flights. He repeated his stunning performances later in the month, and in early June, the wind pushed his plane into a telephone pole during landing. While he was unharmed, it took two days to repair his plane.

Rivals Christofferson and Walsh were constructing their airplanes simultaneously on the Vancouver Barracks polo field camp. But they were

Aviator Charles "Fred" Walsh soars in an exhibition over a Wenatchee, Washington aviation field in June 1911. *Library of Congress.*

not alone. "A score of a dozen mechanics are at the aviation camp on the polo grounds that carry their own forge, tools and materials needed for repairs," *The Columbian* reported.

Walsh got his aircraft in the air first over Vancouver, beating Christofferson and the others, piloting a Curtiss-Farman-Walsh biplane with propellors behind the pilot in June 1911, circling it two to four hundred feet above the Vancouver Barracks. *The Columbian* described Walsh's flight as successful and reported that it extended from the polo grounds over the city, saying, "There was not a moment during the whole flight that the big machine was not under complete control of the skilled aviator." However, the noisy fly-about stampeded the Army mules, and a mother and her children scattered at Walsh's airplane noise.

Two weeks later, Christofferson made his attempt but broke his shoulder in a crash, falling from about thirty feet. The same day, his competitor was testing a piece of new equipment designed to make flying safer. The Ellsworth Equilibrator balanced the wings during banking, claimed its Portland inventor, Dighton G. Ellsworth. Walsh attempted three flights around the polo field, completing only one circle, oddly finding his engine lacked sufficient power to complete the others, although seeming to operate as he expected. This flight rose only fifteen feet above the ground.

By the end of June 1911, the newspaper was showing local readers the transportation technology of the twentieth century concentrated in one place:

> *An audience at the polo grounds viewed three artificial means of transportation, air, water and earth, all within a radius of 100 yards. As Walsh flew his Curtiss biplane, the SP&S train crossed the trestle south of the field, and a clumsy boat rowed by four boys slid across the flooded backwater on the field.*

The newspaper story added a boy struggling to learn to balance his boat, several polo players atop their mounts and a speedster to flesh out the image. "All watching Walsh's flight, one of the steamships that cruised the Columbia River was the only transport missing," the newspaper concluded.

Walsh exhibited throughout Oregon, Washington, Idaho, Wyoming, British Columbia and Nebraska into the autumn of 1911. Some of these destinations had never seen an aircraft. His relationship with the Pacific Aviation Company began to disintegrate during the Nebraska exhibition. First, Walsh and his wife, Alice, suspected they were not receiving 40 percent of the gate as promised. Alice charmed her way into buying tickets one night in Kearney, Nebraska, finding they'd received only half of the promised money. One story goes that the couple decided to face the Mannings the following day. Instead, they found Walsh's plane and the flying field deserted.

However, a story in an Omaha newspaper suggested Walsh crashed into a cornfield during the Nebraska exhibition in Fremont and had to send for a new plane. The angry audience blamed him for giving a poor performance. Worse, Arthur Johnson, the cornfield owner, sued the Pacific Aviation Company for $100 in lost crop, possibly the first such lawsuit. The plane damage forced Judge Hollenbeck to lawfully seize the wreck until the case was settled. (This may be why the broken plane disappeared.) Pacific Aviation resolved Fremont's aviation committee's $300 case on August 24. Walsh sued the Pacific Aviation Company for $56.25 in event ticket sales. The litigation sparked terrible animosity.

Walsh and Manning fought that night outside the Terry Hotel in Fremont about Manning deducting airplane repair fees from Walsh's ticket sales. Walsh said this breached his contract. However, Walsh did not own the plane, the local newspaper stipulated.

Walsh moved his family to Chicago to fly for the Curtiss Exhibition Company. Lincoln Beachey, another Californian, also worked for that group. Walsh was reassured that his plane wouldn't be stolen because the exhibition company owned the planes he'd pilot. Manager Jerome Fanciulli said that if the three went on a tour of the country, he'd give each a new, colorful Curtiss Exhibition machine.

During the 1911 Chicago meet, Lincoln Beachey, Glenn Martin and Charles Walsh, who were all excellent California pilots, were to form a group called the Golden State Trio. Fanciulli said that they'd make good money if they did aerobatics in formation with their planes. None of their competitors, not even Orville and Wilbur Wright, had anything like the three fliers in their exhibitions. But Glenn Martin turned it down, so the "Golden Gate Trio" died. Instead, Walsh and Beachey worked together.

As a result of flying with Beachey, Walsh became a more daring pilot. When he crashed at Trenton, New Jersey, in October 1912, his plane was locked in a spiral; he plummeted from an altitude of over two thousand feet to his death in front of an audience of six thousand. His last resting place is next to his mother in Calvary Cemetery, San Diego.

An *Eagle and Times* news story posits that before Walsh's crash, a future president, Woodrow Wilson, was the next passenger in line for Walsh to take on a fly-around. Walsh, however, instead wanted to make a test run around the field. That run was his undoing but perhaps saved a future president of the United States.

Left Big Apple Society: Walter Edwards Kittel (1880–1922)

Estranged from his parents and fleeing their posh New York City Riverside Drive home, Walter Edwards Kittel dropped his last name and took up flying during his early years of aviation. (Perhaps coincidentally, he hid behind the same name as a silent film actor of the era.) Before turning to flying, Edwards, like his father, was a banker and vice president of the United States Exchange Bank of New York until its purchase in 1907.

Then he traveled to California, demonstrating his aerial skill throughout California and the Pacific Northwest, crashing so often he claimed to have fractured every bone in his body. For a while, Edwards based his flying efforts at the Vancouver Barracks aviation camp, where he competed with other early aviators, including Silas Christofferson and Charles Walsh.

In 1912, the U.S. Post Office granted Edwards a temporary postal route, #673001, and recorded as U.S. pioneer air mail flight #48. Although other intrastate airmail flights had been made earlier in New York, this route became the first sanctioned airmail flight in the Pacific Northwest and the first interstate airmail flight in the nation. (Lincoln Beachey's flight seven years earlier from the Lewis and Clark Exposition to Vancouver Barracks parade ground wasn't post office approved.)

The mail delivery was part of an exhibition held at a Portland country club. The audience there was assured that the airmail flight would be the only thing that interfered with Edwards's performance. The promotion promised he would execute a "series of spiral glides, death dips and other feats of daring" in the same airplane Silas Christofferson floated off Portland's Multnomah Hotel. A "game of aerial baseball" was one of Edward's stunts. From one thousand feet, he'd lob out baseballs and oranges, and whoever below could catch one got a prize. When Edwards tossed the palm-sized spheres, they sped earthward exceeding the speeds of ball thrown by modern baseball pitchers, more than ninety-five miles per hour.

Former banker turned daredevil pilot Walter Edwards Kittel sits in the airplane Silas Christofferson flew off a Portland hotel for the PNW's first exhibition airmail flight. *Oregon Historical Society.*

Rough signs declared the fledgling mail service open for business. Special commemorative stamps were created to cancel the first airmail traveling between Portland and Vancouver. Although scheduled to leave Waverly Golf Links at 4:00 p.m. on Saturday, August 10, 1912, the flight was thirty minutes late. Last-minute postcards and letters swamped the Portland postal system. Some batches were addressed to President Taft, Woodrow Wilson and Teddy Roosevelt. Edwards flew the mail route again on Sunday, August 11. (Oddly, he's not credited for what may have been the first Sunday mail delivery in U.S. history.)

Leaving late from the postal substation at the golf course, Edwards made the first sanctioned interstate airmail flight carrying five thousand letters to the barracks polo field. The Portland letters were postmarked "Portland Aviation Station No. 1." Upon their arrival, the Vancouver postal carriers finished their delivery. For his part, Edwards joked, "No dog will trouble me."

One letter from Portland Mayor Allen Rushlight went to Vancouver's Mayor C.S. Irwin. Irwin responded with suitable diplomacy, "Through the courtesy of Walter Edwards, I return the compliment," and offered best wishes to Irwin's administration. He also mentioned the letter's delivery took only twelve minutes.

Weeks later, a New Yorker exposed Edwards's name ruse at a Seattle hotel when he shouted "Kittel" at him. After some pressure late into the night, Edwards finally broke and admitted dropping his last name, claiming he was done with the shallowness and idleness of high society. When a reporter went to the Kittels' Riverside Drive home and asked if they had a son named Walter, the mother answered they had a son but not by that name, which shows the extent of their split from Edwards.

Flying in Centralia, Washington, in January 1913, Edwards crashed before a crowd of five hundred. He failed to see a telephone wire. As he pulled out too late, his plane's wing clipped the wire, flipping it over. The crowd rushed to him, imagining they'd find the flier dead. He tried to escape but fell thirty feet, entangled in wires, causing bruises and sprained ankles.

Edwards married Grace Wauchope in 1912. After the crash and until his death, he seems to have retired from flying. Before dying at forty-two, he owned a car and taxi service in Washington, D.C. While his wife was away visiting in Hammondsport, New York, his heart failed one evening on his way to the phone to call her. He fell dead against a railing at his home.

A WEDDING ALOFT AND EMIL KOMM (1891–1928)

Weddings and aviation in Vancouver made news throughout Washington State for months in 1911. Life in local communities often creates curious interconnections, sometimes at the county fair. However, conducting a wedding at the county fair was odd.

The Claussen-Stanley wedding announcement didn't seem anything but ordinary. The bride had it printed tastefully, although in torturous Germanic script reminiscent of the Gutenberg Bible. Unravelling the script, the reader finds Henry H. Claussen and Nina C. Stanley were to be married in Vancouver on Saturday, October 7. Obviously, this was but one of many ordinary nuptials that year. Then one's eye catches the smaller, easy-to-read modern print in all capitals at the lower left-hand corner, declaring:

"AN AVIATION WEDDING 1000 FEET ABOVE THE EARTH."

In the early days of aviation, this was the equivalent of getting married during a Superbowl halftime today. Arranging either would be attention-getting, costly and difficult to negotiate. Nothing is mentioned about where the pair might lift aloft from. At the time, the Vancouver Barracks parade and polo grounds were just amateur aviators in tents.

Among thousands of aerial enthusiasts, the two Vancouver lovebirds agreed to rise one thousand feet and wed. According to Polk's 1911 directory, Henry lived at 512 West Main Street and was a driver for Vancouver Soda Works. Because women lived with men or with their families, Nina's address is harder to pin down using Polk's. Only two addresses would seem to fit, Ira Stanley at 200 West Sixteenth Street or Newell Stanley at 715 Eighteenth Street.

Henry and Nina imagined dreamily lifting off the ground as two individuals and then romantically floating suspended between heaven and earth, exchanging vows, trading rings, kissing and descending bound as one in marriage. Likely their initial thought of nuptial vehicle was a balloon, not an aeroplane. Most planes of the day struggled to lift two people into the air. For the ceremony, their clergyman would need to be a wing walker. We do not know how deeply their idea was considered, but at least it smacked of modernity, and the Claussen-Stanley marriage was at the forefront of aviation events. Would this aerial wedding ever float in the clouds?

To the uninformed, a balloon might seem sensible. In a balloon, the yet unwedded might squeeze a minister and a witness into the basket. Balloons had been flying for more than a hundred years. Hot-air balloons had lifted from Vancouver before. Although none rose to the thousand feet the invitation proclaimed. While no balloon had made it to one thousand feet in the local skies, a balloon wedding seemed more reasonable than having the ceremony in an airplane. How the bride would enter and exit the balloon basket gracefully wasn't explained.

Was an aerial wedding even valid? Before lawyers determined the wedding's legal status, more couples signed up for airborne nuptials. Days before the October 7 wedding date, the bride wanted assurance her nuptial knot would bind the two partners as tightly as a wedding on the ground. Newspapers across the state broke the news about the wedding. For example, the October 3 *Spokesman-Review* carried an article about whether an aloft wedding was even legal, suggesting the bride may have been having second thoughts herself:

> *The legality of the aviation wedding to take place in a balloon at the Clark County harvest show next Saturday has been questioned and several of the leading attorneys of Vancouver differ on the question.…The question of the legality of the ceremony was first brought up by Miss Stanley, who wanted to know that the knot would be tied as good and hard as it would be if the wedding took place in a church. When asked, the county attorney, Fred W. Tempes, said he would look up the point. It was a new one to him. James P. Stapleton, former county attorney for four years, said that the ceremony would be Illegal, and to make the marriage ceremony legal and binding it would have to be performed again on terra firma. He gave as his reason that the license was issued to be used in Washington and no other place, and if the couple were married in a balloon, they were not In Washington. It is likely that the matter will be taken up with the state attorney general at Olympia before the ceremony takes place.*

The threat of the state attorney general declaring the legality of in-air marriages soon deflated. The law didn't stop it. The lack of a balloon did. Officials of the Clark County Harvest Days (the name of the county fair that year) couldn't secure one. They could offer an airplane made by Emil F. Komm, an amateur aviator. For several years before World War I, Komm appeared in local papers explaining his inventions.

Komm built a monoplane made from bamboo and weighing 120 pounds. He called it the lightest he'd ever created and turned it into a glider by removing the engine. After removing the engine, the would-be aviator had his bamboo aircraft towed behind an automobile at the polo field air camp, where it lifted three feet off the ground. Despite its light weight and 180 feet of wing surface, the Santo-Dumont-Blériot never flew. Still, Komm told a *Vancouver Columbian* reporter on the scene, he planned to fly it at the upcoming Clark County Harvest Fair. The thirty-horsepower engine was too small to lift the plane, and the inventor intended to use a sixty-horsepower engine.

Komm planned to give free exhibitions every day at the Harvest Fair that October. Although it's unlikely that Komm's plane ever flew under its own power. At the fair, it was the backdrop for the Claussen-Stanley wedding. First Presbyterian Church Reverend H.S. Templeton presided over the ceremony. Without leaving the earth, the pair exchanged vows with Komm's unusual screw-prop airplane as a ceremonial backdrop.

In 1912, Emil Komm sought to prove the efficiency of a small gasoline engine on a sort of airplane-car machine. It flew with wings on. Wingless, it rolled along the roadway as a three-wheeled, thirteen-foot-long car, two wheels under the engine and one in the rear. For three months, Emil Komm, "the young aeronaut of Vancouver," spent his nights and Sundays off working past midnight in a cellar. The vehicle needed to be disassembled to remove it from his basement.

He tested airplane-glider Komm 1 at the Bagley Downs Racetrack (now the location of Eleanor Roosevelt School) accelerating to thirty miles per hour at half-throttle; when pulled behind an automobile it glided fifteen feet above the ground. The driver sat in the vehicle's body, which was constructed

> *like a coffin and offers practically no resistance to the air. The propeller is changed from the driver's seat. On the soft racetrack at the county fairgrounds, Komm did the trio in two minutes with the engine only open 25 percent yet reaching 30 miles an hour on the level ground. Circling the track, Komm said he felt his control slipping so he stopped the engine just as a control wire snapped, spilling him and pinning him in the car. Without wings the car weighs 200 pounds but the wings add little more.*

During an attempt in 1913, as reported by the *Oregonian*, Komm partnered with Bryan Fry to put his efforts into an "Airauto." The machine rolled down Eleventh Street before Fry turned the engine wide open, "flying along the pavement" at fifty miles an hour. An unfortunate dog ran out to chase the unique propellor-driven car, only to be crushed under a wheel, bouncing the car two feet off the ground. Fry used similar designs to skim along the surface of the Columbia River riding on pontoons. The inventors promised more trials, which appear to have been ignored.

That December, Komm advertised his plane for sale in *Popular Mechanics*. Whether it sold is unclear. Komm, however, joined the Army as a private and served at Kelly Field Aero Squadron 327 during World War I. After his 1928 death, he was buried in the Tahoma Cemetery in Yakima, Washington.

Early Navy Flier: Louis Barin (1890–1920)

At 250 pounds, Louis T. Barin was a big man, overflowing the cockpit of his airplane. He was easily twice the weight of the youthful aviators working at the polo grounds aviation camp. But he was there every evening. Later, Barin would make his mark in aviation by becoming one of the first naval aviators. He was likely the last nonmilitary pilot to fly from Pearson Airfield before World War I.

Barin attended Pacific College, learning pharmacy. (There is some question about whether he was a pharmacist or a dentist.) After graduation, the flying bug bit him, and he started building and trying to fly his own airplanes. Barin contracted with the Oregon National Guard as a private and received an honorable discharge in the same year. Five years later, in November, he joined the Oregon Naval Militia (ONM).

A 1910 window display at clothing retailer Meier & Frank (bought by Macy's and closed in 2017) in downtown Portland advertised a model airplane contest that hooked Barin on flying. He didn't win; his friend Danny Grecco did. When first building planes, Barin failed several times. One even flew, sort of. It rose twenty feet from the ground before nosing into the earth. He cut these failures into firewood and stored the scraps in his Portland basement.

During the summer of 1915, the Portlander worked two months building an airplane there. When he completed it, he flew over Vancouver several times. He frequently made flights from the Vancouver Barracks in 1913 and 1914. As the *Oregonian* reported, Barin's aircraft "skimmed Portland's Nob Hill district, later taking a higher level as he flew toward the Columbia River."

A few days later, Louis held an exhibition flight at the Rose City Speedway, lifting off from Vancouver and flying low over Portland in the early evening. On the flight, he dropped "numerous small cards," including four hundred complimentary tickets advertising the following week's racing events and flights. According to the newspaper, the ticket number dropped to three hundred a week later. His craft had only one seat, and anyone wanting a flight annoyed the hefty pilot.

John Burkhart from Albany, Oregon, designed Barin's first airplane and built the first airplane in Oregon in 1910. Burkhart had an engineering degree and some aviation training at Cornell University and had made his own plane two years earlier. Burkhart was a technical advisor to the Army in World War I and often advised other pilots while flying out of Pearson Airfield. Barin and his mechanic, W.T. Baily, built the plane.

In December 1911, Barin and D.D. Harding and his wife were paddling a canoe on the Willamette River when a motorboat hit it, tipping it over. Mrs. Harding entangled her foot in the canoe's seat, and Barin rescued her, helping her board the speedboat. The boat owner, E.A. Lamberson, helped those overboard and towed the canoe to Ross Island, where Harding declared he'd have Lamberson's boating license revoked.

Lieutenant Louis T. Barin dressed in his naval officer's uniform. He piloted the NC-1 flying boat that attempted a 1919 transatlantic crossing and crashed in the Azores. *Wikimedia Commons.*

Local newspaper reports say the Oregon-born Barin spent three years and $3,000 refining his monoplane in Portland and hauled it to the barracks to fly for weeks. His plane skittered across the grass without gaining airtime. The Portlander came every evening to the polo field to attempt flying and returned home to Sixth and Ash in Portland on the 6:00 a.m. ferry. Finally, it made a few short hops off the ground.

He received offers to make flights at fairs and one to fly with automobiles at the Rose City Speedway. But needing a more powerful engine, he declined to go. His present engine was too dangerous in turns, and Barin hoped to buy a one-hundred-horsepower engine. With his current engine, he'd flown at seventy-five miles per hour and raced trains passing along the edge of Pearson Field.

Once Barin had a pilot's license, he wished to create an aviation corps in the Oregon Naval Militia. To convince several officers of the Oregon National Guard, he flew his aircraft at Vancouver Barracks polo field in January 1916. The officers ruled his exhibition a success. They noted Barin's fitness and athletic ability would suit him serving as an officer in the nascent aviation corps—if he could drop to 190 pounds, a challenge he met. Barin was the last of the early aviation pioneers making up the aviation camp to fly out of the polo field before World War I.

Impressing the Oregon Military Department staff with his piloting and weight loss, Barin served on the ONM staff until July 1916, when he gained a commission as an ensign. The ONM placed him in charge of the emerging Aviation Corps of the Oregon Naval Militia at the rank of chief mechanician.

Orders came in early 1916 for Barin to attend the Aviation School in San Diego. Curtiss Aeroplane Company, which was closely tied to the Navy, paid his tuition. He was to participate long enough to get his naval pilot license and then proceed to the Naval Aeronautic Station Pensacola, Florida.

Drawing on his experience, Barin worked as an instructor for the Naval Aeronautic Station, training over one thousand Navy pilots. He also tested new aircraft for the Navy. His intrepid flying ability earned him the nickname "Daredevil Barin." As if reinforcing that nickname, he was the first pilot to fly loops in a seaplane with pontoons.

During World War I, Barin taught aeronautical theory at Pensacola Flight School. Assigned to the Naval Air Station at Rockaway, New York, after World War I, Barin flew Curtiss H-12 and H-16 seaplanes. Once, when he was in an experimental aircraft at six thousand feet, the plane turned over and began to fall. Barin kept his head during the speeding descent, trying to regain control. He wrenched back control of the beast a few hundred feet above the water. His goggles and helmet were gone when he landed, and the force of the rapid descent from that altitude shredded his clothes.

On three attempts to cross the Atlantic in 1919, he copiloted the 126-foot-wingspan Curtiss NC-1 "flying boat" that held a crew of six. He performed navigation duties as a crew member on the flying boat that finally made the crossing. The Navy promoted him to lieutenant in the U.S. Navy Reserve that June. On the final Atlantic crossing Barin flew, he made it as far as the Azores, when the aircraft was forced to land in fog so dense it obscured the island's high peaks. He landed the flying boat on twelve-foot-high waves too rough to allow him to take flight again. The impact damaged the aircraft, which sank while being towed by a rescue ship.

When an Army flight cadet, Joseph Walker, hit Lieutenant Barin's high-speed test plane in midair over the San Diego naval airfield, the lieutenant died instantly, and his mechanic received serious injuries. Although unable to avoid the crash, Walker escaped injury. The *Tacoma Ledger* and newspapers around the country noted Barin was "one of the most experienced fliers in the Navy" and mentioned his piloting an Atlantic crossing in the Curtiss NC-1. He was awarded the Navy Cross posthumously for his participation in the flight from Newfoundland to the Azores. Portugal gave him the Portuguese Military Order of the Tower and Sword for that flight.

3

ARMY SKIES

With the United States' April 1917 entry into the First World War, most flying stopped except Forest Patrol searching for forest fires at what would become Pearson Field. In 1922, the Army Air Service formed the 321st Observation Squadron at the Vancouver Barracks led by Lieutenant Oakley Kelly. The Vancouver Barracks Aerodrome (later renamed Pearson Field) saw the advent of the 321st as the beginning of a new era in military aviation. To teach Army Reserve officers flying, Lieutenant Kelly used four Curtiss JN-4 Jennies and one DeHavilland DH-4. The reserve unit remained at Pearson until 1941, when the squadron was activated by the U.S. Army Air Corps. During this time, Pearson served as an intermediate field within the wider network of the Air Corps' eleven bases.

Spruce Cut-Up Plant: Wood for War Planes

World War I shifted airplane manufacturing from the hands of passionate self-designers and kit builders to the assembly line. During the war, a Spruce Mill Cut-Up Plant operated by the U.S. Army Signal Corps covered a large portion of the formerly grassy polo field. It transformed raw spruce timber into the lumber other plants milled into the lightweight spruce ribs that kept the Air Corps and Allies in the sky. Built in ninety days, the plant would eventually employ thousands of soldiers. Between 1917 and 1918, it is believed the United States produced raw materials for nearly fourteen thousand aircraft.

The Spruce Mill was a first and brief attempt by the United States to run a government manufacturing plant. Interestingly, only one-third of the mill's output was allotted to American aircraft factories, with the remaining two-thirds delivered to the Allies. During wartime, aviators still innovated, perfecting techniques for aerial photography and mapping, crop-dusting and forest patrols. The mill was in operation just eighteen months, and the Army destroyed it soon after the war's end.

Although airplanes had yet to be used in combat, as the United States inched toward entering World War I, the War Department considered airplanes critical for the success of the war. With the frameworks of planes made of wood, they needed a tree to win the First World War—the Sitka spruce. It had formed airplane bodies and wings since aviation's early days because its wood possessed the unique qualities of durability, strength, flexibility and lightness. Early airplane builders, including the Wright brothers, discovered it difficult to find spruce.

The red spruce found in the northeastern forests didn't grow to the heights needed for the long ribbing required in an airplane. Only the Sitka spruce, which grows in a fifty-mile-wide band along the Pacific Northwest coast, was knot-free and tall enough. When the United States joined the Allies in World War I, the military understood Allied airpower depended on building airplanes with Sitka, and it needed to protect and control the flow of raw material.

At the time, the Northwest forests crawled with the anti-capitalist International Workers of the World (IWW), or Wobblies. While committed to nonviolence, some Wobblies favored socialism and a few anarchy. Wobblies were often accused of sabotage, starting forest fires, slowing workflows or breaking equipment. Yet they championed better wages and safer working conditions in all trades, making some see them as socialists, even communists. They organized logging camps. Business management and local law officers frequently came down hard on any union activity. At Everett, Washington, special anti-union deputies massacred thirty-one union members on Bloody Sunday in 1916, which increased federal concerns about logging labor stability.

Bloody Sunday and Wobblies in the woods worried General John "Black Jack" Pershing and Secretary of War Newton Baker, as did the constant reporting of German spy activity. An Iowa newspaper reported a rumor, denied by the commander of the Vancouver Barracks, that a German spy had been shot there. The Army worried that strikes by the IWW might cripple their attempts to build airplanes. To counter the Wobblies, the lumber industry resorted to patriotic advertising and publicly accepted the eight-hour day the Wobblies supported. The Army seduced Brice Disque (1879–1960), a former Army captain, to reenlist and head up the Spruce Production Division (SPD). The new division would manage the forests and logging and settle the disruptive labor conditions that might hinder the war effort. The Army took over lumber production and quelled labor unrest for the first time. Disque often joked, "He came to see and stayed to saw."

Disque began his career soldiering in the Philippines and rose through the enlisted ranks to captain before leaving the Army. He arrived in Portland in the fall of 1917 to lead the SPD, then part of the Army Signal Corps. To begin his mission, Disque toured Pacific Northwest lumber camps, finding loggers working under harsh conditions but often less radical than the IWW, which was organizing lumbermen and other

General Brice Disque erected the Spruce Cut-Up Plant in just ninety days to mill spruce for World War I airplanes. *Oregon Historical Society*.

workers by demanding an eight-hour-day, higher pay and safer working conditions. In just ninety days, Disque built the Spruce Cut-Up Plant (between today's Pearson Museum and the Fort Vancouver replica). The plant sawed spruce logs that went to other mills, where the timbers were turned into the framework for warplanes. His involvement was the first example of the early twentieth-century collaboration between industry and the military affecting labor.

Returning from the tour, Disque concluded he'd solve the labor turmoil with soldiers—and adopting some of the IWW's goals. He'd also create a competing and more patriotic union, the Legion of Loyal Loggers and Lumbermen, or 4L. The 4L would give loggers what the IWW wanted, safer working conditions and military-quality sanitation at the camps. By improving camp life, building mills, paying soldiers civilian wages and instituting the eight-hour day, he'd dull the IWW's efforts. These decisions, he believed, would keep the spruce flowing. Controversy swirled around Disque's changes. However, he knew that by offering much of what the Wobblies sought, logging camp morale would improve.

Controlling the 4L and the SPD, Disque gained unprecedented power over a lumber industry previously lacking organization around the production of airplane-grade spruce. Loggers usually worked twelve-to-fourteen-hour days but had been striking for the eight-hour day. Disque shifted to the shorter day in March 1918 and said he would assign SPD soldiers to the camps that complied. These steps soothed the labor situation. Still, existing sawmills couldn't meet the demand. So, he'd construct a big one near the railway along the Columbia River.

Disque hired Oregonian H.S. Mitchell to oversee the building of the cut-up plant at the Vancouver Barracks, the world's largest, covering fifty acres. The plant produced enough raw material to build three hundred planes a day. In ninety days, Disque erected the nation's largest mill to shape spruce, called the Spruce Cut-Up Plant, at the Vancouver Barracks, which, after logging, was the first link in the chain of processes to turn trees into airplanes.

SPD officers came from various Army branches. The first 105 officers arrived in Vancouver from the San Francisco Presidio five days after Disque gained command on November 15, 1917. Disque assigned 12 officers to recruit Loyal Legion loggers and mill workers in Washington's camps and mill towns. These new recruits were primarily recent graduates of the Officers' Training Corps. As newly commissioned officers, they had civilian business and managerial skills but no military experience.

Although many may have preferred the front lines of France, the officers were placed in remote locations in the woods along the West Coast from California to the Canadian border. New troops arrived at Vancouver and dispersed where they were needed. On December 4, five thousand enlisted men were reassigned by the Army and were sent to work as hook tenders, choker setters, rigging slingers, loaders, knotters, signalmen, firefighters, engineers and graders across California, Oregon and Washington.

Vancouver supervised the plant, which ran twenty-four hours a day; transportation; and guard squadrons and provisional companies. Plant production began in January 1918 and sawed nearly 10 million board-feet of spruce a month. Before the end of the war, it had milled 76,653,429 feet of lumber, with some going overseas to Britian, France and Italy. About 30 percent of the lumber didn't meet aircraft quality standards but was recycled for other commercial uses.

The World War I Source Mill in Vancouver, Washington, was the largest in the world and milled Sitka spruce for first stage of airplane production. *Fort Vancouver National Historic Site.*

The guard squadrons were conventional troops on garrison duty at Vancouver Barracks and available to respond to problems such as strikes, sabotage, fires or natural disasters like forest fires or floods. They were used to fight burning forests in August, September and October 1918. The summer of 1918 was noteworthy for its fire season. More than 300,000 acres of public and private timber burned, and as much as 3 billion board-feet of timber was destroyed. The soldiers who logged or worked as mill workers were seen as cowards by many. Others felt the combined military pay and logging pay SPD soldiers received was unfair.

By 1918, the mill had reached the required total of 10 million board-feet a month and 22 million by the war's end. The war was over twenty months after America joined the Allies against the Germans. By then, Disque's staff included 30,000 SPD soldiers and 125,000 4L members, some former IWW members. Moreover, in eighteen months, the plant produced 143 million board feet, an increase of 1,700 percent, while heading the SPD.

SPD Newspaper

The SPD developed its own trade publication, *Straight Grain*, named for the plant's straight grain cuts in the Cut-Up Plant. It was written, edited and published by the SPD soldiers, and its graphics designer was an already well-known artist, Lewis Grell (1887–1960), an SPD soldier.

Grell made his first *Straight Grain* appearance twelve days after Armistice. A headline about demobilization reported that a lack of forms was slowing the process. The November 30 issue carried his first signed art, two humorous drawings. One covers nearly half a page, explaining how to succeed as a sergeant.

After his discharge from the Army, Grell returned to Chicago and his art career. Grell married Fredricka Seammers, a woman he met in Europe, taking wedding vows at the Tree Studio Building in 1922. He won the Henry Frank prize in 1930 and the Municipal Art League prize in 1936.

The artist's mural clients included movie theater architects and hotel chains. This work explains why he is primarily considered a muralist, and several of his murals exist today, including at the Chicago Theatre. However, his work was broader, and his family collection includes still lifes, landscapes, mural studies and portraits. As Chicago's Tree Colony members, he and other artists entertained celebrities at the Tree Studio Building. He returned to teaching in 1940 at the Academy of Fine Arts. While teaching, he continued as a muralist until his death.

A postcard of artist Lewis Grell (*right*), dressed in a World War I Army uniform, standing with another soldier, likely at the Vancouver Barracks, in 1918. *LouisGrell.com*.

Effects Beyond World War I

Disque might have been a war hero. But politicians intervened, prompted by the disgruntled workforce in the lumber business. An estimated ten thousand Allied planes were built with American spruce. Approximately one thousand American DH-4s made it to Europe, largely to England. Starting in August 1918, an estimated two hundred may have been flown during combat in France. The House Subcommittee on Aviation wanted to know why and called Disque to testify, questioning each decision he'd made. In the end, the panel cleared him but sullied his reputation and left him disillusioned.

In 1919, President Wilson, authorized by a 1918 Act of Congress, presented the Army Distinguished Service Medal to now Brigadier General Brice Disque for his exceptionally meritorious and distinguished services in a duty of great responsibility during World War I to the U.S. government for the organization and administration of the Bureau of Spruce Production under War Department Order 69. By World War II, Disque was working in the energy industry.

When World War I ended, the need for airplane spruce dried up. After Armistice Day, the Cut-Up Plant shut down. The leftover lumber was sold off by sealed bids by the Spruce Division. Almost $10 million of equipment was also sold. The four thousand men running the Cut-Up Plant left the Army. The 4L members decreased. The last soldier in the SPD was released. By 1924, the ground under the plant had returned to its original state.

When General Pershing returned victorious from Europe, he found his country planting memorial trees honoring the 117,000 Americans who died overseas. Among his first acts was planting a tree in New York's Central Park, one of several he planted. Each memorial tree was also an unacknowledged salute to the tree that won the war.

After World War I, Disque questioned the waste of the SPD, including an incomplete Port Angeles mill and $4 million railways in Washington State completed too late to use. So, leaving the Army, he used his contacts to obtain a position in industry on the board of G. Amsinck & Co. Inc. of New York. During the 1930s, he involved himself in the coal industry by accepting executive positions at Pittston Coal Company and as the lead person at the Anthracite Institution and a trade association for coal producers in Pennsylvania.

The Army recalled him a second time in 1941, installing him as associate director in the Office of Solid Fuels Coordination, which ensured coal supplies for both military and civilians. Once again, his work caused controversy, and the army asked him to resign after fifteen months. After his final resignation, he returned to the coal business, heading the Coal Consumers Protective Association until he retired in 1957.

Working with the coal and lumber industries turned him sour on unions. For history, the collaboration between the Army and the 4L began a flow of information between the military and labor that shifted the civilian economy of the so-called free market. Disque's efforts illustrated how to suppress radical unionism, a concept corporations would later advance.

During World War I, what remained of the flying field was left for a few airplanes used to spot forest fires. With the closing in 1918 of the Cut-Up Mill, the airfield was used mostly by civilians. Around 1921, a cooperative relationship between the Air Service and the Forest Service formed the Army's forest patrol for tracking the woods for forest fires.

321st Reserve Squadron

The polo fields south of Vancouver Barracks served as a temporary landing strip for civilian pilots in the early 1900s. While private aircraft were allowed to land at Vancouver Barracks, it wasn't until 1921, after World War I, that military aircraft began modestly using the facility for operations, when the U.S. Army Air Service established a landing field for an aviation forest patrol. At first, the U.S. Army and U.S. Forest Service worked together on patrols to locate forest fires in Oregon and Washington.

When Vancouver Barracks joined the U.S. Army Air Service program in 1922 (renamed the U.S. Army Air Corps in 1926), the Army constructed an airstrip to support air reserve training and sent the 321st Observation Reserve Squadron to the barracks, where they remained until World War II. When the squadron arrived at the barracks two years later, in 1924, the station had just three biplanes. The 321st was a reserve training unit that conducted reconnaissance missions and combat simulations. When apple orchards in Oregon were infected, the team was called in for an emergency crop-dusting to save them.

When Lieutenant Oakley Kelly took command of the unit in 1924, he was one of the armed services' most well-known pilots and a transcontinental record holder with Lieutenant John Macready. Under Kelly's leadership, the Army upgraded Pearson Field's infrastructure, making it one of the most

Members of the 321st Observation Squadron pose for a group photo at Pearson Field in 1926. *Fort Vancouver National Historic Site.*

modern military airfields on the West Coast. He ordered the leveling of the grass field and the construction of several hangars between 1924 and 1926.

In 1925, Lieutenant Kelly expanded the field to accommodate airmail aircraft and newly established commercial carriers, freight and passengers. He also sponsored record-breaking flights and encouraged Vancouver civilian pilots as part of his efforts to enhance aviation in the Pacific Northwest. What had been polo fields was named and dedicated as Pearson Field in September 1925 with an air show to honor Lieutenant Kelly's friend and well-known Army aviator Lieutenant Alexander Pearson Jr., who had recently died in an airplane accident. Lieutenant Oakley Kelly led the squadron until 1929, after which Lieutenant Aubrey Eagle took over.

Lieutenant Noel B. Evans's life illustrates how pilots frequently switched between military and private flight. The Army assigned Evans to Pearson Field in 1925 after he completed his pilot training with the 840th Aero Squadron at Camp McArthur, Texas. Prior, he attended a military aeronautics school in Austin, Texas, as well as a flying school in Southerfield, Georgia, and an army aeronautics school in Austin.

Evans was with the 321st Observation Squadron at Pearson Field from 1925 until April 1932. While in the Northwest, Evans served as a relief pilot for Pacific Air Transport, flying planes between Portland, Seattle, San Francisco and Los Angeles. He then served as a copilot with West Coast Air Transport. Evans flew three-motor Fokker monoplane transports from Portland to San Francisco in 1930, when Western Air Express bought West Coast Air Transport. Evans left the Army and the Northwest in January 1932 to work as a pilot with Varney Speed Lines, which operated flights between San Francisco and Los Angeles. He perished when his plane crashed in severe weather in 1933. At his death, Evans had logged over 4,200 flight hours.

Throughout the 1930s, the 321st carried out training activities. Until December 1941, the unit remained a reserve force stationed at Pearson Field. After the bombing of Pearl Harbor, the Army activated the 321st, halting all military activity at Pearson Field. Several structures from the 321st era exist, including the ordnance storehouse east of the Pearson Air Museum, the historic hangar south of the museum, the headquarters building that held Lieutenant Kelly's and later commanders' offices, as well as the grass field and runway.

Under Kelly's leadership, at least one noncommissioned officer (NCO) flew. Usually, NCOs were mechanics. Enlisted NCOs, usually staff sergeants or above, piloted planes during World War I under the 1916 National Defense Act, later revoked. In September 1923, the Army again permitted physically fit NCOs "between twenty-two and thirty years old" in the Officers Reserve Corps to enter flight school at Brooks Field, Texas. Soon after this order, Lieutenant Kelly and James Powell, commanding Pearson Feld, each listed an unidentified staff sergeant as a pilot in a training and operations report for February 1923 and July 1924.

Shown here in his flight gear, Lieutenant Noel Evans is an example of a pilot who moved easily between military and civilian commercial aviation. *Fort Vancouver National Historic Site.*

CROSS-COUNTRY RECORD HOLDER: LIEUTENANT OAKLEY G. KELLY (1891–1966)

In an era of routine less than six-hour coast-to-coast flights, it's difficult to imagine the first one took nearly twenty-seven hours. On May 2, 1922, an Army Fokker T-2 airplane left Mitchell Field, New York. It flew 2,625 miles before landing the next day in San Diego. The two pilots, Lieutenants Oakley Kelly and John Macready, set the record for a U.S. transcontinental flight. For that, they won the 1923 Mackay Trophy, awarded for the "most meritorious flight each year," and in 1924 the Distinguished Flying Cross.

Around the same time, the Vancouver Barracks polo field was morphing back into an airfield. In 1921, polo field Army pilots were still taking to the skies to spot forest fires, as they had during World War I. In 1921–22, when the barracks merged with the U.S. Army Air Service program (later the Army Air Corps), the Army located its 321st Observation Squadron there under Second Lieutenant Laurence Barrett Hickham.

The holders of the fastest cross-country trip record showed up at the Vancouver airfield. Lieutenant Macready arrived in 1923. The polo field served as a base for him and a photographer to shoot local aerial pictures that helped map Vancouver's port, giving locals the first aerial pictures along the Columbia River. Then, the War Department sent Kelly in February 1924 to turn the dual-use polo flying field into a bona fide military airbase.

The same year, the Army commissioned an around-the-world flight with four customized Douglas World Cruisers, hoping to beat other nations to the record. With the planes scheduled for arrival in Vancouver, Kelly and others flew to Eugene, Oregon, to escort the world travelers here and on to Seattle.

Kelly knew the flying field needed enlargement and old planes required replacement. To extend the flying field, he leveled the Spruce Cut-Up Plant. When a pilot unable to gain sufficient height to avoid the Interstate Bridge (erected in 1917) dunked his plane in the Columbia, it proved Kelly's decision correct.

Kelly also expanded aviation by tirelessly promoting flying and exhibiting a knack for finding events that captured public attention. He used the daredevil in him to encourage aviation and thought nothing about flying under the Interstate Bridge. He piloted ninety-four-year-old Ezra Meeker east to Washington, D.C., over portions of the Oregon Trail so the pioneer might meet with President Coolidge about preserving the way West. Together they covered Meeker's four-month trek in just four days, clocking twenty-four hours of airtime.

Lieutenant Oakley G. Kelly at Pearson Field, where he commanded the 321st Reserve Squadron. *Oregon Historical Society.*

When Vancouver convinced Congress to mint a fifty-cent piece for Fort Vancouver's centennial, Kelly achieved another first by retrieving the coins from the San Francisco mint, flying round trip from Vancouver to San Francisco in a record ten hours and fifty-five minutes—returning the coins in time for the celebration.

The Fort Vancouver Centennial Corporation sold stock to get the centennial rolling but was forced to shut down in April 1925. It had planned to raise funds with the coins. What promoters had hoped to be a significant event fell through, and they abandoned the centennial in April, according to the *Vancouver Columbian*. The causes cited were financial problems and public apathy. As it turned out, local enthusiasts, including history aficionado Glenn Ranck, revived the centennial on a smaller scale. In August, just two weeks before the event would start, Ranck and others knew they needed to excite the public about the anniversary of the fort. As a publicity stunt, Kelly flew the first round-trip flight from Vancouver to San Francisco and back on the same day carrying 1,462 pounds of coins—two weeks before the event would begin.

According to Kelly in an exclusive article for the *Oregonian*, newspaperman and Centennial Committee President Herbert J. Campbell asked the pilot one Friday midafternoon to fly immediately to the California mint and bring the commemorative coins to Vancouver in a rush for the centennial. Kelly thought it over and proposed making the trip in a single day because the San Francisco mint would be closed when he arrived otherwise. (Kelly was perhaps also a bit opportunistic and saw a way to add another "first" to his list of aviation accomplishments.) They decided Kelly would leave the following morning. The one-day round trip would grant added importance to the commemoratives by adding a unique aviation event—the first round-trip flight between the two West Coast cities.

Without breakfast or coffee, Kelly left Pearson Field at 5:15 a.m. for the trip, stopping along the way as necessary to refuel. His passenger was the editor of the *Portland Journal*, Don Sterling. At 11:35 a.m., they arrived in San Francisco. There Kelly signed for the fifty thousand coins and ate breakfast. At 12:30 p.m., he headed back to Pearson Field, making the 1,400-mile round trip in ten hours and fifty-five minutes. The same photo accompanying both the *Oregonian* and *Vancouver Columbian* articles shows Kelly by his airplane between Campbell and Mayor B.E. Allen. Campbell is handing the first Fort Vancouver commemorative half-dollar minted to the mayor as a uniformed policeman stands nearby with a high-powered rifle at port arms, proving the coins were well guarded. The first twenty coins were placed in numbered envelopes for local dignitaries. The mayor was to deliver the ceremonial coin to President Coolidge. The balance went to Warren Howard, a vice president of the Vancouver National Bank, who handled and distributed them.

Kelly knew the flying field needed enlargement and the aged planes replacement. Focused on updating the flying field, Kelly built a new $6,000 hangar, improved roadways and graded the grounds. He spoke with local clubs, fraternities and the chamber of commerce, convincing locals of the importance of aviation and the benefit of an airfield in the town.

He also championed airmail and passenger air service. Kelly supported, scheduled and flew in air circuses, even dropping tickets from his plane to encourage attendance. In between these activities, he sometimes flew to go fishing. Kelly presided over the airfield and the squadron until 1928, when Lieutenant Aubrey Eagle stepped in.

FLIGHT TO SAVE THE OREGON TRAIL

On October 1, 1924, a begoggled ninety-four-year-old Ezra Meeker waited in the U.S. Army De Havilland DH-4 for Kelly's arrival. The lieutenant would fly the Washington pioneer over the Oregon Trail that brought him west as a young man. The youthful lieutenant and the crusty pioneer circled the airfield before turning east. Ezra Meeker (1830–1928) was on his way to becoming the first cross-country air passenger. Even at one hundred miles per hour, he urged Kelly for more speed. So, the pilot called him the original "let's go man." Knowing that the press was watching, Meeker shrewdly sent telegrams between cities where he touched down, allowing newspapers to track his progress.

The first day, Meeker's eight-dollar hat blew away. On the second, strong headwinds made for a bouncy ride. After gas stops in Wyoming, they landed at Fort Cook near Omaha, where reporters wrote Meeker jumped from the plane "as spry as a man of 40." Falling short of Indianapolis the next day, Kelly landed at Chanute Field near Rantoul, Illinois. The day after, they landed at Dayton's Wilbur Wright Field. When escorted to the grandstand, they faced 100,000 cheering air show spectators, and Meeker did his first radio interview. When Meeker and Oakley landed in Washington, D.C., the ninety-four-year-old finally delivered his message to President Coolidge, urging him to approve all the Oregon Trail projects. In six days of cross-country hops, Kelly flew over territory that seventy-five years earlier Meeker traversed by oxcart in five months.

Mrs. Oakley Kelly says goodbye to Ezra Meeker, who's waiting for Lieutenant Kelly to fly him over the Oregon Trail to Washington, D.C. *Oregon Historical Society.*

FIRST AROUND-WORLD FLIGHT, 1924

Escorted by five Curtiss JN-4s from Pearson Field, four specially outfitted Douglas World Cruisers stopped in Vancouver on St. Patrick's Day 1924 on their way to Seattle to start their transglobal tour. Mayor Allen closed all government offices so employees could join the enormous local crowd, including Portlanders crossing the Columbia River. Even the Prunarians, a local business group supporting Clark County's prune industry, showed up in uniform. Holding a crew of two, each cruiser, painted yellow and green, bore a symbol—two soaring bald eagles and a globe encircled by the words "Air Service U.S.A. World Flight." The specifications for each of the four Douglas World Cruisers were:

Length: 35 feet, 6 inches
Height: 13 feet, 7 inches
Wingspan: 50 feet
Powerplant: 1 Liberty V12 engine, 420 horsepower
Maximum Speed: 103 miles per hour

The four planes bypassed Portland because it lacked an airfield large enough for the planes. Named the *Boston*, *Chicago*, *New Orleans* and *Seattle* for cities representing the nation's regions, the cruisers landed at Pearson for servicing and refueling before hopping to Seattle's Lake Washington, where they would start their circumnavigation on April 6. Five European countries and Argentina also hoped to beat the Americans but would fail.

The open cockpit cruisers carried 2,700 pounds of fuel, leaving 3,000 pounds for equipment, a pilot and a mechanic. Piloting over the sea meant carrying pontoons. Extra parts were taken for quick repairs. To keep the planes light, parachutes and radios were left behind.

Army logicians mapped the route by breaking it into legs, the shortest 100 miles and the longest 830. They set up well-equipped repair and supply depots. Seven could handle major overhauls, even swapping out engines. The 175-day, 27,000-mile flight kept to the Northern Hemisphere, never crossing the equator.

Fragile aircraft, tricky navigation, bad weather and icebergs became the enemies of success. To skirt the worst weather, the planes flew west over Alaska and then down the Asian coast, ultimately stopping in twenty-eight countries and making seventy-two stops for fuel and maintenance.

Two of the twelve-cylinder cruisers were lost. The *Seattle*'s pilot misjudged low ground and crashed into an Alaskan coastal mountain near Miller Point.

The Army crews wearing protective flight gear for warmth for their flight from Sand Point, Washington, before they started around the world. *National Air and Space Museum.*

Although their injuries were minor, it took the pilot and mechanic, Major Frederick Martin and Staff Sergeant Alva Harvey, several days to walk through snow and fog to safety.

The *Boston* lost its oil pump and set down in a turbulent sea near Iceland. After a rough landing, the sea tossed the craft around with the pilot and mechanic as they waited for help. Hours later, two destroyers pulled alongside. While the plane was lifted with a sling, an immense wave pitched up the *Boston*, crashing it into the crane. The ship's captain worried towing the aircraft would sink his ship and ordered sailors to chop holes in the *Boston*'s pontoons. After flying twenty thousand miles, the *Boston* dipped below the North Atlantic. It would be resurrected later as the *Boston II* and complete the flight.

On September 27, 1925, a record holder of the first transcontinental flight across the United States, Lieutenant Oakley Kelly, and six more Pearson pilots flew to Eugene, Oregon, to escort the *Boston II*, *Chicago* and *New Orleans* to Seattle. But when the oil pump of *Boston II* failed, the World Cruisers landed an unexpected second time at Pearson Field. The stop was unscheduled and caught Brigadier General Kuehn, commander of the Vancouver Barracks, by surprise, making him rush to the field to greet the fliers. The needed repair halted plans for a Portland reception of the around-the-world fliers the following week. Within thirty-five minutes, the oil pump had been swapped out, and the fliers headed for Seattle, with Lieutenant Kelly continuing to escort the three planes on the last leg of the transworld flight.

The cruisers' around-the-world flight time was 363 hours and 7 minutes. After the quick repair at Pearson Field, the planes flew in V formation from the airfield and then headed to Sand Point Field to avoid the Seattle throng awaiting them, completing the first circumnavigation of the globe by air. Later, Congress voted for the airmen (except Martin and Harvey, who lost the *Seattle* in Alaska) to receive the Distinguished Service Medal—the first time it had awarded it for nonmilitary action.

Appearing before a congressional investigation committee in January 1925, Lieutenant John Harding and Lieutenant Leigh Wade argued for the need to launch a commercial aviation industry and night flying using beacon lights on mail routes. Early in the same day, Dwight Davis, secretary of war, made a similar plea about the need for a commercial airplane business. That year, Houghton Mifflin published *The First World Flight*, by Lowell Thomas, traveler, radio commentator and writer. The book told the narrative of the fliers—Lowell Smith, Erik Nelson, Leigh Wade, Leslie Arnold, Henry Ogden and John Harding. Thomas had written stories for the press during the last portion of the historic flight.

As for Pearson Field, it served two more celebrated military flights before World War II. Just four years later, the first Russians would land there, followed by the Russian transpolar flight in 1937. Both brought international attention to Vancouver.

MYSTERIOUS KLAN FLIGHT

A flight over the Clark County fairgrounds in August 1924 celebrated the Ku Klux Klan Klavern No. 1 of Clark County. The Klan sponsored an event promising fireworks, carnival fun and a flying "flaming cross," a mainstay of Klan intimidation against its enemies. The cross turned out to be not fiery but illuminated. At dusk on a humid August evening, a biplane dangling a lighted cross bearing the letters KKK flew above thousands at the Clark County Fairground.

An Army Reserve noncommissioned pilot looked down at the thousands looking skyward from what was then the largest event ever held in southwest Washington. The Klan event recruited more than one hundred new disciples. At the time, Clark County had a negligible African American population. So, the Klan pitted Protestants against Catholics instead while framing its bigotry in patriotism, family values and law and order.

The thousands of attendees at the Clark County Fairground (at Bagley Downs) were thrilled when an airplane flying high over their heads suspended a fiery cross above. The crowd was exhilarated by the plane's "series of spectacular convulsions." Before the Klanvocation concluded, the Invisible Empire inducted one hundred "citizens" in front of thousands of spectators. (The Vancouver Klan's first public naturalization ceremony occurred the previous summer.)

Vancouver, Washington, wasn't the only place the KKK employed aircraft. Klansmen also piloted planes and dropped hate literature from the skies. *Library of Congress.*

Most of the KKK officials from the West Coast, Georgia and Washington, D.C., attended. Hundreds of Oregon Klansmen crossed the Interstate Bridge to bring their families and sympathizers. Observers counted two thousand automobiles at the fairgrounds. Klan estimates of attendance spiked at forty thousand. The *Vancouver Columbian* reported ten to fifteen thousand people. By either count, it was the largest Klanvocation in the Northwest.

For one hundred years, no one knew where the flight originated or who flew the plane. But the Army did, as uncovered in materials from the National Archives. A local businessman, James Clancy, proprietor of Pioneer Job Printing on Main Street, sent a letter to John Weeks, the secretary of war, dated August 24, and another to the commanding officer of the barracks. Each called attention to the Klan flyover the day before. Clancy simply asked who authorized the Vancouver Barracks field for the Klan flight. His single-sentence letter prompted a rapid Army response for investigation; it mentioned the "demonstration has attracted considerable unfavorable comment." In short, the Army was embarrassed.

Investigation responses by the commanding officer and Lieutenant Kelly tell the same story. The Oregon, Washington and Idaho aviation field on the Willamette River was "temporarily unavailable" for commercial flights because of hydraulic dredging. Starting in June, Lieutenant Kelly allowed commercial flights to shift to the Army's Aerodome. Among the pilots who shifted to the Army's field was Vern Bookwalter, a commercial pilot and an enlisted reserve corps sergeant. Bookwalter received one hundred dollars to make the August Klan flight dangling an illuminated cross from the aircraft. National Archives documents show neither Kelly nor Bookwalter received punishment stronger than reprimands for the humiliation the Army suffered over the flight. Joseph Kuhn, commanding officer, wrote that while sharing the Army field for commercial flights was a good policy, he prohibited "commercial aviators from staging any flights from this field which may be considered in any way as furthering religious, racial or political propaganda, under penalty of being denied the courtesy of the field."

Still, mysteries persist around Bookwalter's "flaming cross" flight. How was the cross constructed and illuminated? How did he take off and land with it? Did he have help?

Twice Field Commander: Carlton Foster Bond (1893–1980)

Visitors to Pearson Air Museum often mistake the bronze statue by the walkway for Pearson Airpark's namesake, Alexander Pearson. Looking closely at the bronze plaque, they learn the figure is Carlton Foster Bond. The statue was placed in 1996 to celebrate Bond, who was twice commander of the airfield, as a lieutenant from 1929 to 1932 and as a captain from 1939 to 1942. His career moved him from an enlisted foot soldier to the longest-serving commanding officer of the 321st Observation Air Squadron stationed at Pearson Field.

The Chicago-born Bond's command at Pearson Airfield was forgotten. Neither his 1980 death notice nor his obituary in *The Columbian* mentioned the forty-three-year Vancouver resident's two tours of duty at Pearson, although they mentioned his affiliation with the Masons and St. James Catholic Church and recognized him as a retired Air Force colonel.

In 1916, Bond served as an infantry sergeant along the Mexican border chasing outlaws and fought the battle of the Rio Grande. He was one of the few aviators who were also balloonists and held free balloon license number 863. The first mention of him in the area was in 1917, when he attended a six-week ordnance class at the University of Oregon. After graduating from pilot school in 1918, he gained an officer's commission and, by 1920, his pilot's license. Bond also held an airship pilot and observer ranking. In 1922, he served in several European countries. From 1926 to 1928, he was in the Philippines.

He competed as a copilot in the 1922 Gordon Bennett Balloon Race in Geneva, Switzerland, where he took off and drifted 490 miles in about seventeen hours into Hungary. After lifting 35,000 feet over the Alps, he and his pilot cracked a valve to lower its altitude, rapidly dropping the balloon 18,000 feet. Reacting to lift the balloon, they pitched out empty oxygen tanks, carefully avoiding civilians below. Like small bombs, the tanks exploded on impact. Their effort lost the dragline. The blast made the Hungarians think they started a war. Suddenly, the balloonists felt a jerk; looking down, they saw two hundred angry Hungarian peasants pulling the overboard balloon rope. Grounding the balloon, the peasants pulled the two from the basket, ending the race for Bond and Major Westover. When the gendarmes arrived, they were hauled to the calaboose, which disqualified the balloon for being on the ground for more than fifteen minutes.

In 1929, Bond took charge of Pearson Airfield and the 321st Reserve Squadron. By then, it was among the premier Air Corps bases on the Pacific coast. Pearson Airfield had a mix of airplanes, including Curtiss JN-4s (Jennies), DeHavilland DH-4s and Consolidated PT-1As. By 1930, modern aircraft had appeared, including PT-3As and Douglas O-2H and O-38 planes. Bond made flights to retrieve both repaired and new planes to keep the airfield's inventory operational and current.

Although he was responsible for training, he also liked to keep the men busy and flying. In 1930, Bond arranged a flying baseball team, creating the Pacific coast's first air-minded ball team. In July, nine aviators flew begoggled up the Columbia Gorge to Prineville, Oregon, where they outscored the Prineville nine 7 runs to 4. "We're going to fly other places and play. It's a great way to go to a ball game," Bond told an *Oregonian* reporter.

During his first stint at Pearson, commercial flights expanded. Portland and Vancouver wrestled over who would be the area's future commercial airport. The field had two side-by side runways, one for the Army and another for commercial and airmail flights, called Chamber of Commerce Field. Deeper-pocketed Portland eventually won the commercial contracts for Swan Island Airport, decreasing the importance of Pearson Field. Swan Island was finished in 1930 in time for Charles Lindbergh to land there, snubbing Pearson.

From foot soldier to balloonist and then aviator, Captain Carlton Foster Bond was twice the commander of Pearson Field and during his first tour commanded the 321st Observation Squadron. *Clark County Historical Museum.*

In 1929, the all-metal *Land of the Soviets* ANT-4 made a surprise landing at the Army's Pearson Field on October 18. A pump on the Russian bomber broke down. Aviation mechanics of the 321st Squadron at Pearson repaired the pump overnight, allowing the Russian fliers to leave the next day for San Francisco, the next leg of their Moscow to New York flight.

When Russell Cunningham, an airmail pilot, went down with wing icing in 1931, Bond and the 321st searched for him. Cunningham safely hiked out. However, a Varney Airmail pilot, Walter Case, wasn't so lucky. Last seen flying east toward Pasco, Washington, he died in a crash in rough country. For a week, the *Vancouver Columbian* covered the search for his body on its front pages. Varney aviator Russell Voorhees located the wreckage from the air. The following day, four Washougal hikers stumbled on the wreckage in the pass between Silver Star and Big Baldy mountains. Forest rangers spent a grueling thirty-five hours transporting Case's body down off the mountains. A Varney official, Leon Cuddeback, declared it the worst crash he'd ever seen.

Bond also flew supplies to a remote Geodetical Survey team near the North Fork of the Lewis River at Skookum Meadows. The crew had snowshoed into the mountains to conduct studies of the Columbia River and its tributaries. He'd drop supplies wrapped in old *Columbian* newspapers and then return a few days later to see if the men wrote "OK" in the snow, signaling they'd received the supplies. He flew around the Pendleton Rodeo with aerial photographer Burton Thurber, taking photos, and then flew those and other photos from the rodeo to the *Oregonian*—195 miles in 1 hour and 25 minutes, an average speed of 138 miles per hour. Thurber told the *Oregonian* that even at 1,000 feet above the rodeo, he smelled the hamburgers and hot dogs, but speeding back along the gorge he smelled forest fires.

During Bond's second Pearson tour in August 1940, a bomber from the 73rd Bombing Division fell out of the sky at Kalama, Washington, north of Vancouver. Bond received a message from McCord about an unconfirmed crash of a bomber last heard from near Portland. That December, he hosted Major General Henry "Hap" Arnold, who was on an inspection tour of air units in the West. On his December 1940 visit, he claimed he wanted to see what was going on. While here, he recalled the days when he led the forest patrols from Pearson Field. (Later, Arnold and Jackie Cochran would create the WASPs, Women's Air Force Service Pilots.)

Bond served at other air bases, including Hawaii; Kelly Field, Texas; and Lake Charles, Louisiana, where he organized a fighter gunnery school, and commanded a heavy bomber base in Salina, Kansas. During the Second World War, he spent time with a task force on an unnamed Pacific island. Although the records seem unavailable, Bond transferred from the Army to the Air Force after Congress created it with the National Security Act of 1947. He retired from the Air Force as a colonel and lived in Vancouver for about fifty years.

EARLY MILITARY PLANES

Curtiss-JN-4 Jenny

In America's interest in military, civilian and commercial aviation, the JN-4 is undoubtedly the best-known World War I aircraft. The Glenn Curtiss Aeroplane Company of Hammondsport, New York, later known as the Curtiss Aeroplane and Motor Company, created the Curtiss JN "Jenny" series of biplanes. The JN-4 was built by the Curtiss Company in 1914 and 1915 and then produced in huge numbers during World War I. Although the Curtiss JN series was initially designed as a training aircraft for the U.S. Army, the "Jenny" (a nickname derived from JN) continued to be built after World War I as a civilian aircraft, becoming what many aircraft historians recognize as the "backbone of American postwar [civil] aviation."

An estimated 95 percent of pupils trained in JN-4s, a dual controlled, two-seater biplane with the student sitting in front of the instructor. Its tractor propeller and mobility made it ideal for initial pilot training. The 90-horsepower Curtiss OX-5 V8 engine delivered a max speed of 75 miles per hour and a flying ceiling of 6,500 feet. The V8 engine was solid but underpowered. Still, Jennies were the first planes to deliver mail on a regular basis and worked admirably, but postal officials

The Curtiss Jenny taught America flying. Barnstormers flew from town to town demonstrating their expertise and offering rides for a fee, often only making gas money. *Aeronautical Division, U.S. Signal Corps.*

worried their small motors and flimsy fuselages could not stand the long-term daily operation required.

When the United States declared war on Germany in April 1917, the Army was rushing to educate thousands of pilots for the war effort, and it required a basic aviation trainer that could accommodate both an instructor and a student. Curtiss's JN design proved to be a great match, and the company was commissioned to manufacture approximately six thousand planes. This biplane, like the larger DH-4 bomber used by U.S. forces, featured a wooden frame covered in fabric. Its frame was made of Sitka spruce, and the need for spruce led to the establishment of the U.S. Army's Spruce Production Division at the Vancouver Barracks (now Fort Vancouver National Historic Site). Much of the spruce gathered at the Vancouver Spruce Mill was used to construct JN-4 and DH-4 aircraft in Ohio and New York.

Following World War I, many were sold to civilians, flooding the market. Wannabe fliers bought thousands of surplus Curtiss Jennies at a discount after World War I. They sold for as little as fifty dollars each (some still in their original packing crates). Even Charles Lindbergh bought one in May 1923 and soloed in it. With no restrictions on private or commercial flying in North America, pilots discovered that the Jenny's stability and slow speed made it ideal for stunt flying and aerobatic displays.

Most aviation enthusiasts consider the Curtiss JN-4 Jenny part of aviation's barnstorming era. Barnstorming was how many early pilots funded their flying. One or more would land near a small town running some festival or fair and offer ten-minute rides for $10 (nearly $170 today). Others see it as the plane that taught Americans how to fly in both the First World War and during the 1918–25 peaceful period that followed. Between the world wars, famous fliers, including Edith Foltz, barnstormed in the Jenny, flying into a community and selling tickets for rides, to earn money to fund their flying habit.

In September 1926, the army stopped flying all types of JN aircraft, and the remaining Jennies at Pearson Field were stripped of their engines and other critical equipment, heaped up and burned unceremoniously. Today, Pearson Air Museum has a volunteer-built Curtiss Jenny on exhibit.

De Havilland DH-4

British aviation engineer Geoffrey De Havilland designed the DH-4 and initially flew with the British Royal Flying Corps in early 1917. When the United States entered the war in April of that year, one sample was provided to see whether it was suitable for American production. The DH-4 Liberty became the only American-built plane American forces used in World War I combat.

In July 1917, the American Aircraft Production Board approved the construction design using an American-designed V-12 "Liberty" engine, making the American DH-4 planes known as "Liberty planes." Due to a breakneck manufacturing schedule, the first Liberty airplane rolled out of an American facility on October 29, 1917, six months after the United States entered the war.

The DH-4 aircraft's Sitka frame was covered in fabric and hardened. The first DH-4 Liberty aircraft landed in France on May 11, 1918, after being

A Liberty DH-4 like this is among a handful in the world and is exhibited at Pearson Air Museum at Fort Vancouver National Historic Site. *Department of Defense.*

flown by training crews from the United States. During the Meuse-Argonne campaign in the fall of 1918, the aircraft performed superbly, carrying out strategic and tactical bombing flights against German targets. By the November 1918 Armistice, 1,213 Liberty aircraft had been sent overseas for combat. Between October 1917 and the end of the war, the United States built 4,846 Liberty aircraft, a staggering total in little over a year. Following the war's end, the DH-4s established the Army Air Service's fleet of combat-ready aircraft and frequently flew in early airmail runs. Pearson Air Museum visitors can see a DH-4 Liberty plane. Interestingly all the DH-4s in Europe cost too much to return to the Unites States, so their engines were pulled and their bodies burned.

4
PEARSON FIELD'S ROLE IN EARLY AIRMAIL

A French balloonist, Jean-Pierre Blanchard, crossed the English Channel to deliver a single letter to France in 1785. In 1793, he delivered the first airmail in the United States, a letter from President George Washington.

Just a year before the Civil War broke out, John Wise, loaded with 120 letters, ballooned from Lafayette, Indiana, headed for New York. Foul weather forced his landing just twenty-five miles from his liftoff point. From then on, bad weather assaulted deliveries throughout the early days of airmail flights.

Pearson Airpark appreciably contributed to the evolution of airmail. Lincoln Beachey rose from the Portland fairgrounds at the Lewis and Clark Exposition on September 19, 1905, flying across the Columbia River. He set his sausage-shaped dirigible *Gelatine* down on the barracks parade ground as awed Vancouver residents watched. The eighteen-year-old pulled several letters from inside his jacket and handed them to the postal clerk, Win Carson, who lugged them to the Fourth and Washington Streets post office. He also carried a message addressed to General Constant Williams, commander of the Department of the Columbia.

In 1912, the U.S. Post Office granted the Portland Post Office a temporary postal route, #673001, for an exhibition run. This route became the first sanctioned airmail flight in the Pacific Northwest and the first interstate airmail flight in the nation. Rough signs at both ends declared the airplane mail service open for business. Walter Edwards piloted a pusher plane (the propeller was behind the pilot) on the weekend of August 10 and 11. He carried five thousand letters postmarked "Portland Aviation Station No. 1" to the barracks field.

Six months before the end of World War I, airmail service in the United States began. A letter sent by President Woodrow Wilson was among the first batch. At first, Army pilots flew the routes. Rates were twenty-four cents an ounce but quickly dropped to sixteen cents. Still, the public shunned such costly rates.

Expensive rates opened the airmail service to entrepreneurs like Vern Gorst and Walter Varney, who used Pearson Field for their airmail transport companies, Pacific Air Transport and Varney Air Mail. Both companies flew only West Coast routes.

During the 1920s, pilots lacked radios, flight instruments, landing lights, direction beacons and flight towers. They flew by intuitive "dead reckoning" or by following highways, railroad tracks or rivers. There's a rumor some pilots created crude altimeters by somehow anchoring a half-empty pint of whiskey to the dashboard to keep the plane's wings level.

Pilot inexperience caused many crashes. However, the death toll remained low because early planes were slow, maneuverable and landed in any open space—a golf course, beach or pasture. Still, thirty-four airmail pilots died between 1918 and 1927 from capricious weather and undependable equipment.

While Lincoln Beachey and Walter Edwards pioneered airmail delivery between Portland and Vancouver, Beachey's 1905 airmail flight was an unofficial event and Edwards's was an exhibition, albeit one the local postal office sanctioned. By the mid-1920s, airplanes carrying cargo had moved from the exhibition stage to commercial ventures, first in mail transport and then passengers. But while Pearson Field would be involved in these early stages within a little more than a decade, it would fall to its competitor on the south side of the Columbia River, Portland.

Six years after Edwards's flight in May 1918, America launched the world's first regularly scheduled airmail service in the midst of the First World War. That day, U.S. Army pilots flew mail for the Post Office Department between Washington, D.C.; Philadelphia; and New York. President Woodrow Wilson signed an envelope that was among the first pieces of airmail carried. It was addressed to the Honorable T.H. Patten, postmaster, New York City, and carried the first U.S. airmail stamp. Noah W. Taussig, president of the

American Molasses Company and avid philatelist, arranged for the creation of a special envelope for this flight. Once the envelope was stamped by the post office, he urged the president to sell it, giving the proceeds to the Red Cross.

President Woodrow Wilson and First Lady Edith Wilson holding the first official airmail letter in 1918. The letter was auctioned off for $1,000, which was donated to the Red Cross. *Library of Congress.*

Several things attracted nascent airmail services Pacific Air Transport (PAT) and Varney Air Mail to Pearson Airfield. There were few other landing places on either side of the river at the time. Pearson's flat area, located along the Columbia River, allowed pilots to easily find the field by following the waterway. Additionally, the Army was building new hangars and maintaining the landing field, at least in the early days. The Interstate Bridge toll caused second thoughts about airmail, because vehicles, horses and mail trucks had to pay a five-cent toll to cross. However, the nickel toll was eliminated before the end of 1926 for mail vans and for all vehicles in 1929.

In February 1925, Congress passed the Contract Air Mail Act, allowing the U.S. Post Office to award private airlines contracts to deliver mail by air. The law also supplied money to make the airmail routes safe to fly, even at night.

Varney Airlines: Walt Varney (1888–1967)

During World War I, Walter T. Varney flew for the U.S. Signal Corps Aviation Chapter. After the war, he was a flight teacher who also ran an air taxi service. Varney envisioned delivering cargo and mail by air and bid on an airmail route from Pasco, Washington, via Boise, Idaho, and finishing in Elko, Nevada. Some claimed the 460-mile path went from "nowhere

Walter Varney was an aviation air transport pioneer whose early efforts became the forerunner of two major U.S. airlines, United Airlines and Continental Airlines. *Wikimedia Commons.*

to nowhere," but Varney expanded his airline up and down the West Coast. He bought six Swallow biplanes; each could transport six hundred pounds of mail.

His chief pilot, Leon Cuddeback, flew the first contract postal trip in the Pacific Northwest from Pasco, Washington, to Elko, Nevada, on April 6, 1926. He carried six bags of mail weighing over four hundred pounds to destinations all over the Pacific Northwest. Lieutenant Oakley Kelly and a contingent of aviators took off from Pearson Field to participate in the ceremony. Mail from Vancouver arrived at Pasco by train that day.

The first airmail flight for Varney Airlines from Pearson Field to Pasco, Washington, lifted off on September 1926 in a 1,600-pound Stearman Speed Mail plane capable of 145 miles per hour. Morning mail stops were at Pearson and evening at Swan Island. The flight was to originate from Swan Island, but fog delayed the flight, although *The Columbian* poked at its rival Portland, touting that Pearson Field was "bathed in sunshine," when in reality it was rather dim sunlight.

Competitors Varney Airlines and Pacific Air Transport worked together if one of their pilots was forced to land. In 1927, Vern Bookwalter took off from Pearson Field, picked up mail from a Varney airplane forced to land and flew "special delivery" from Vancouver to Seattle.

Varney sold out to United Airlines in 1930 and founded Varney Speed Lines with a partner, Louis Mueller, in 1934. Varney sold that line to Continental Airlines.

PACIFIC AIR TRANSPORT: VERN GORST (1876–1953)

A successful Klondike gold seeker, Vergne "Vern" C. Gorst directed his golden gains toward flight in 1913. Before that, he dabbled in transportation, creating a boat motor launch service, an automobile business and several West Coast bus lines. With an eye to the future of transportation, he watched the brothers Wright closely, even naming his son Wilbur. When Silas Christofferson flew off the Multnomah Hotel, Gorst was among the crowd watching. Later he paid for flights with the famous pilot.

Gorst incorporated Pacific Air Transport in January 1926 and sold stock. Among his shareholders was Julius Meier, owner of Meier & Frank. A Wells Fargo loan officer, William A. Patterson, helped Gorst get funds and became his advisor and eventually president of United Airlines after its purchase of Gorst's business.

In late 1925, PAT received a government contract to deliver regular airmail. Gorst selected Pearson Airfield to service the Portland Post Office for the Seattle to Los Angeles route because, at the time, Portland lacked a viable airfield. However, whether Pearson Field was used as a regular stop is unclear. It seems to have been an alternative to Swan Island while the Portland airport was under construction, shrouded in bad weather or other no-fly circumstances.

PAT owner and president Vern Gorst stands to the left of Claude Ryan, manufacturer of Ryan airplanes used for airmail runs, after completing a 1926 survey of Gorst's West Coast route. *Oregon Historical Society.*

On September 15, 1926, PAT employee Vern Bookwalter flew the first government-sanctioned airmail round trip for Gorst's service and returned, making his cargo the first official U.S. Postal mail transported between Oregon and Washington. In 1919, Army flight instruction gave Bookwalter four hours of training before he soloed. That earned him pilot's license No. 82, signed by Orville Wright, which he proudly displayed. Two years earlier, he flew over the Clark County fairgrounds toting an illuminated cross for the Klan.

Stunt pilot Tex Rankin nicknamed the "well padded" Bookwalter "Anti-lift," defining the term as "a large unnecessary object holding an airplane down." Unhampered by the nickname, Bookwalter flew his Ryan-M1 monoplane from Pearson Field at 5:25 a.m. with 184 pounds of mail headed for Medford, Oregon, landing three hours later. He exchanged the Ryan for a Travel Air to return to Pearson with ten mailbags. When he arrived at 11:30 a.m., a crowd of six thousand locals greeted him. His landing marked the third time letters were delivered to Vancouver by air.

Piloting planes modified to hold cargo was dangerous, not because of the load but because of the schedules that had to be met. Fog, wind, inclement weather and night flying caused delays and more than an occasional crash. Two of the northern route's eighteen full- or part-time PAT pilots died in crashes.

ARMY DELIVERS THE MAIL (AGAIN)

The Air Mail Act of 1930 eliminated competitive bidding. Instead of a flat rate per mile regardless of the cargo weight, the payment was now calculated based on load weight per mile. Contracts were awarded based on the aircraft's payload, so the more a plane could carry the more it brought in. In 1933, a Ku Klux Klan member who would become an associate justice of the U.S. Supreme Court, Alabama Senator Hugo Black, worried that airmail contracts weren't being awarded competitively but instead given to companies friendly to the Hoover administration. He requested Congress ferret out this fraud and collusion. Black headed the investigation to determine whether the existing contracts might be voided.

Congress authorized the secretary of war to assign military aircraft, landing strips, pilots and apparatus for airmail transportation with the 1934 Air Mail Act. The mandate shifted airmail delivery to the Air Corps. Under General Benjamin Foulois, army pilots unprepared for the assignment flew mail across a reduced number of routes. Locally, this decision meant bypassing Portland's overcrowded Swan Island municipal airport. The Air Corps established its airmail headquarters at Pearson Field, making the field the hub of army airmail activity.

Pearson Field had advantages. For night flying, it had carbide lights. The Corps Reserve forces already occupied the small field with two hangars, a little office and an administrative structure. Twenty-eight enlisted soldiers and twenty-five civilians looked after the planes. The Reserve Air Corps paid a monthly twenty-five dollars for each airplane hangared, and its staff included one officer, three enlisted soldiers and two civilians at the local airport. After an airplane arrived in Portland, it unloaded its mail and took off for Pearson Field for maintenance.

The Air Corps didn't fully commit to Pearson. However, it soon became obvious that the headquarters and maintenance facility would be there, but Portland's Swan Island Airport would be used unless the weather made that field impractical. To fly Pacific Northwest mail, nine Douglas 0-25s with modified cockpits for mail were kept at the field. Pilots flew two routes—Portland to Salt Lake and Seattle-Portland-Boise.

Postmaster General (1929–1933) Walter Brown became involved in the airmail scandal unsuccessfully shifting delivery to the Army. *Library of Congress.*

Regionally, Army pilots flew 43,179 pounds of mail from February to May 1934, covering 97 percent of the 201,326 miles allotted, without losing anyone and with no serious crashes. This was a better record than the corps service nationwide. Several tragic accidents tarnished the Air Corps' reputation, as newspaper articles complained the transition from commercial to military mail occurred too fast. The corps defended itself, saying its pilots were flying during the most dangerous time of year, winter. It claimed Army planes were designed for a couple of bodies, not to haul heavy mail bags. Also, Army pilots were trained to fly in military situations, not at night and in stormy weather.

Eventually, the Swan Island Airport closed and was moved to the east side of Portland, where it would become Portland International Airport (PDX). After the attack on Pearl Harbor, Pearson Field turned into a parking lot for military vehicles. During the war, the hangar that still stands today served as the barracks for about two hundred Italian prisoners of war between 1943 and 1946. Technically, they were not prisoners of war, because Italy had surrendered. Instead, these prisoners were dubbed "cobelligerents."

These cobelligerents wore khaki uniforms with "Italy" patches on the left sleeve. They followed the Army's schedule and discipline while at Vancouver Barracks. Any with specialized skills put them to use for the Army. The rest labored at the barracks, Camp Hathaway and Camp Bonneville doing work the military needed.

Temporarily, after the Second World War, activity at Pearson Field picked up. After all, it had both military and commercial runways. But Swan Island was larger, making the Vancouver airport less competitive. So, the Army shed Pearson Airfield, while still considering it of aviation history importance. In 1949, the City of Vancouver acquired the field adjacent to its commercial field, with the Army maintaining navigation rights.

Airmail had disappeared by 1975, but it officially ended in May 1977, when the Postal Service announced all first-class mail would be transported at the same level of service or better. Stationery aficionados, however, may still find envelopes with "Par Avion" printed on them. The edges of the envelope and stationery are still edged in a blue and red border.

United Airlines Began at Pearson

Pearson Field has two players that might be considered the grandparents of United Airlines—Varney Air Lines and Pacific Air Transport, each founded in 1926. United Airlines absorbed both through a series of acquisitions. VAL operated the first privately chartered air postal flight in 1926, and United Aircraft and Transport Corporation purchased VAL and PAT to enter the airmail business, making the precursor to what would become United Airlines.

Pacific Air Transport's route was more meandering. In late 1925, PAT received a government contract to deliver regular airmail on the West Coast. Vern Gorst, the owner and president, selected Pearson Airfield to service the Portland Post Office for the Seattle to Los Angeles run because, at the time, Portland lacked a viable airfield.

In 1927, Boeing Air Transport was established, later merging with Pratt & Whitney to form United Aircraft and Transport Corporation (UATC). The following year, Gorst sold PAT to Boeing, staying on as an executive. Besides VAL and PAT, UATC additionally acquired Stout Air Services National Air Transport, forming United Air Lines Inc., and entered the transport and passenger businesses. Currently, United

Early air transport from Pearson Field by Varney Airlines laid the foundation for two of America's largest lines. Continental was absorbed by United Airlines in 2010. *Wikimedia Commons.*

Airlines makes about 5,000 flights a day worldwide. This consolidation of several airlines links two early airmail services flying out of Pearson Field to the major airline.

First Airline Magazine

The first airline magazine also has links to Pearson Airport through brother and sister pilots Walter and Ann Bohrer. *Tale Spins!* the magazine was written and illustrated by hand, reproduced using a mimeograph, put in an envelope and mailed. Today, we might call it a "comic book" or a "zine." Think of *Tale Spins!* as a precursor to *Mad* magazine but with content for aviators rather than teenagers.

First published in Portland, *Tale Spins!* was the in-house publication for the Rankin Flying Service, started by the stunt pilot Tex Rankin, who taught flying at Pearson Airfield for about eighteen months in the mid-1920s. The magazine spilled from the creative minds of the brother and sister duo Walt, as illustrator and writer, and Ann, as writer and editor.

They launched their magazine careers with *Tale Spins!*, which sometimes humorously, sometimes satirically, characterized flying. The sibling pilots distributed the first mimeographed issues by hand. The *Capital Journal* in Salem, Oregon, fell back on aviation language, casting Walt as the "pilot" and Ann as the "copilot," flaunting the sexism in the aviation business.

The siblings' effort emerged as America's first humorous aviation magazine, running from 1927 through 1939. The magazine title flowed across the cover in vapory contrails from a tiny plane spinning off to the upper right corner. Although the image flowed horizontally, the magazine's readers knew the plane was out of control, sort of like the humor they'd find inside.

Above the title ran the words "The monkey glands of aviation," a reference to a bogus 1920s medical procedure promising men rejuvenation, longer life, better memory and eyesight. The only rejuvenation the magazine promised was aviation news, gossip and humor.

The pilot and publishing duo took nothing too seriously, including their magazine. It had that "what me worry" kind of idiosyncratic humor. Eventually, *Tale Spins!* became widely read by aviators and outgrew the blue mimeographed ink to find itself in the black ink of print and featuring nationally known pilots or aviation incidents. A twelve-month subscription ran $1.50 ($27.49 today) and included contributions by humorist Will Rogers and pilot Wiley Post, among other aviation celebrities.

Soon, many early airlines carried *Tale Spins!* as their first inflight magazine, including Northwest Airlines, Pennsylvania Central Airlines, KML-Royal Dutch Airlines and Imperial Airlines (today BOAC). Besides being pilots, Ann and Walt Bohrer were aviation writers with an irreverent sense of humor.

When Admiral Richard Byrd returned from his first polar expedition in 1930, Ann and Walt went to hear him lecture in Cleveland. In her oral history, Ann said, "Walt presented him the first copy of our Eastern version of *Tale Spins!*" She mentioned they had been his friend in the past and that he carried their magazine to both the North and South Poles. The

Not knowing the longevity of their funny books, the Bohrers printed early *Tale Spins!* on cheap paper, now disintegrating, like this 1934 copy. *Oregon Historical Aviation Society.*

siblings also gathered up supplies for him that included Pacific Northwest foods, among these one hundred pounds of Tillamook cheese.

Ann and Walt were editing the magazine in Cleveland when they went to nearby Painesville, Ohio, to meet Amelia Earhart, who was on a lecture tour raising funds for her 1937 world flight with Wiley Post. They gave the famous flier their first eastern edition. Earhart signed on as one of their subscribers.

As the Second World War approached, they continued publishing their magazine from Cleveland, but before hostilities they went different ways. Walt moved to California, joining Tex Rankin, who now trained pilots for the war. Ann entered government work with the Fish and Wildlife Service.

Both Ann and Walt were frequent contributors to the aviation press. Walt penned two biographies of Tex Rankin. Then he and Ann penned three humorous books together during the 1960s and 1970s, in the same light vein as their magazine, including *Twenty Smiling Eagles* (Vantage Press, 1962), *Tales Up!* and *This Is Your Captain Speaking* (Aero Publishers, 1971 and 1975). Ann did the words and Walt the pictures. For *Tales Up!*, Ann convinced Douglas "Wrong Way" Corrigan to write the foreword. Corrigan, after a successful transcontinental flight from Long Beach, California, to New York City, was supposed to fly back west. But, directionally impaired, he flew east to Ireland instead, gaining him an unenviable nickname.

For their books, Ann wrote letters to famous fliers, including General James Doolittle, novelist and airline pilot Ernest K. Gann and the actor Robert Taylor. Incredibly, when these fellows wrote back, they confessed that they had no humorous incidents to retell. The siblings dedicated *Tales Up!* to Tex Rankin and their mother, writing that Rankin "taught us, often to appreciate the humor in aviation" and noting their mother "more often than not kept the vast majority of early pilots from starving to death."

5
SOVIETS PART U.S. CLOUDS

There was no Soviet Empire before the Russian Revolution, but there was a vibrant burgeoning aviation interest, including men and women in western Russia. The Grand Duke Alexander Mikhailovich of the Russian imperial family lent prestige and financial support in the early 1900s, often acquiring Fokker and Wright experimental aircraft and sponsoring air races in Russia. Empire pilots participated throughout Europe in air shows and races as early as 1910. This enthusiasm gave rise to several famous Russian aeronautical engineers such as Andrei Tupolev and Igor Sikorsky.

Joseph Stalin, head of the U.S.S.R. Communist Party, wanted to show his country's strength through goodwill with the *Land of the Soviets* 1929 flight. *Public domain.*

Stalin's ascension promised the Soviet people order, wealth, success and international prestige. Stalin issued a series of Five-Year Plans leading to the long-awaited Utopian society. His first one prioritized aviation. Stalin wanted Soviet aviation to surpass the West and modernize the U.S.S.R. The Soviet leader entered an already thriving aviation environment outside the Soviet Union. While flying was still in its infancy, he demanded Russian planes fly "faster, further, and higher" than Western aircraft. Outside the U.S.S.R., many airplanes were still experimental prototypes as the concepts of aerodynamics evolved. Often pilots put their lives on the line. The Army's 1924 around-the-world flight bolstered confidence in aviation, yet only two original planes completed the flight. Then, two Soviet crews did the unthinkable—by flying two bombers to the United States.

First Russian Landing, 1929

In October 1929, the Russians came flying a prototype all-metal aircraft. The transport bomber, *Land of the Soviets*, developed engine trouble shortly after reaching Portland on Friday, October 18, during a trans-Siberian flight from Moscow to New York. On October 19, an *Oregon Journal* story covering the ANT-4 landing listed the crew as Commander S.A. Shestakov, pilot; Philip E. Bolotov, pilot; Boris E. Sterligov, navigator; Dmitry A. Fufaev, mechanic; and Andrew W. Petroff, vice president of the Amtorg Trading corporation, which sponsored the flight.

Print and broadcast media had tracked each leg of the flight from Moscow over the Aleutian Islands to Seattle. From Seattle came word of a Russian landing at 9:30 a.m. on October 18 in Portland. The ultra-long-distance flight was destined for New York City. A quick Portland stop was to refuel and lift off again.

Thrilled Portlanders swooped to the Swan Island Airport to see the Soviet Tupolev ANT-4 twin-engine heavy bomber land. The crowd's excitement wilted when the angular ANT-4 monoplane's ninety-four-foot wingspan passed two thousand feet overhead, banking widely eastward. Not until later did they know engine problems appeared near the airport and the crew shifted to Pearson Field, a U.S. military base, seeking more protection and crowd control for repair.

Meanwhile, at Pearson Field, Army pilots went on high alert. Field commander Lieutenant Carlton Bond and five pilots were now taking off to intercept the huge Russian aircraft and escort it to the military airfield, away from the crowded commercial airport. Bond and his fliers engaged the ANT-4 over Oregon City, chaperoning it to Pearson.

A Portland laundryman, Alex Brillant, also Russian, hoped he might glimpse the plane from his homeland. Sighting the southbound plane turn toward Vancouver, he drove there, supposedly on business. Hurrying to the field, he greeted the Russians in their own language, only to find out one of

The Soviet ANT-4 transport bomber was examined by a crowd at Pearson Field in Vancouver, Washington, on October 18 or October 19, 1929. *Oregon Historical Society.*

the crew, the copilot, Philip Bolotov, was his former playmate. The Army kept Brillant busy the remainder of the day translating for the crew.

The *Land of the Soviets* was on a purported goodwill tour, although the Soviet Union and America had yet to establish diplomatic ties. The head of the Communist Party, Joseph Stalin, wanted to display his country's long-range aviation capability. One-fifth of the U.S.S.R. was arctic, so making trans-arctic flights was a way to test an aircraft in low-temperature conditions and establish new, shorter trade routes.

In limited English, the navigator Sterligov explained he wanted the left engine radiator and faulty oil intake repaired quickly. Other crew members asked for flight and weather charts to speed their takeoff. When interviewed, Petroff contended the long-distance trip was simply to establish trade routes, not for glory or "air-mindedness." *The Oregonian* reported most of the crew was cautious and publicity-shy, shunning hero worship. The crew understood any international misstep would have ended their careers, or worse.

Schools closed, allowing students and teachers to see the big plane. Vancouverites clogged Pearson Field by the hundreds when the ANT-4 landed. The throng examining the aircraft on October 18–19 couldn't believe the colossal, all-metal plane could fly. Repairing the engine took longer than hoped, making the crew stay overnight. They planned to take off at 6:00 a.m. on October 19 to begin the next leg of their flight. But as early as 5:30 a.m., locals assembled at the Army field determined to see the hulking aircraft off. Skeptics saw the ANT-4 smoothly lift from the field headed to Oakland, California, where it landed that afternoon before continuing. After nearly thirteen thousand miles and 137 flight hours, the ANT-4 landed at Curtiss Field, New York City, on November 2, greeted by six thousand New Yorkers.

Second Russian Landing, 1937

The morning of June 20, the roar of an airplane engine woke twelve-year-old Don Carpenter, who could recall the sound of every airplane he'd ever heard. This one was different. Popping from between his sheets, he saw a red-winged plane banking west. He pulled on his clothes and grabbed his bicycle and took off for Pearson Airfield. From the cockpit, three men emerged, wrapped in fur-laden cold-weather attire.

The red and gray Tupolev ANT-25 bomber had traveled just over 5,200 miles to the airpark in slightly over sixty-three hours. But the Soviet plane wasn't supposed to land there. It was flying to Oakland, California.

That June, the Soviet aircraft had flown a route most thought impossible over the North Pole. Cloud banks rose above twenty thousand feet, higher than the ANT-25's maximum ceiling. The crew fought arctic cyclones, freezing weather and ice that thickened to five inches on the front edges of the plane's wings. The crew understood crashing in the desolate arctic made rescue impossible. Safe for the moment, and over Canada, their concerns shifted to the remaining fuel. How much had been spent fighting headwinds, storms and ice?

A water-cooled twelve-cylinder V-engine powered the monstrous monoplane with its red wings spanning 112 feet. Its body hauled two thousand gallons of fuel, enough for a one-hundred-hour flight—more than half the flight's weight of 24,750 pounds. Crew analysis showed they'd not make it to Oakland and might land short. Over Eugene, Oregon, the engine pressure gauge fell. The pilot sent a message that the pump failed, and he'd land at Portland's Swan Island Airport.

Approaching the airport, pilot Valery Chkalov saw mobs of people waving their arms. He passed a note to his navigator telling him to change course and instead land at the military base in Vancouver. He recalled the 1929 Soviet landing chose Pearson over Portland's airport. So, his decision to land at Pearson may have been more intentional than impulsive. And with his crew being military fliers, they were likely to feel more comfortable landing at a military base where they and the ANT-25 would be better protected. Based on the earlier flight, he might have also known what kind of reception he would receive at a military base.

At 150 feet, the plane circled the Swan Island airport. Missing out on a Soviet landing a second time, exasperated Portlanders saw only a flyby. Later, Chkalov explained he feared the Portland crowd ripping apart his ANT-25 like the Paris crowds stripped Lindbergh's *Spirit of Saint Louis*. Although it was the copilot who landed the plane in the grass field at Pearson, not Chkalov the pilot, it would be Chkalov who'd overshadow all the crew members in history.

Charles Alexander was corporal of the guard at the Vancouver Barracks when the Russians landed and offered the story from a military view. He recalled the day as "raining, drizzled, and very foggy." The private on guard saw the ANT-25 and shouted for Alexander, but by the time he dashed from the guard shack, the Russian plane had landed. The Army guards held the Russian fliers up next to the Fifth Street fence, while Alexander called the officer of the guard and General George Marshall's headquarters. In a short time, the duty officer, soldiers and Marshall were all descending on the flying field.

Diplomatic ties between the U.S.S.R. and America were just four years old and fragile. Two days before the landing, the Russians claimed no awareness of a transpolar flight, something they had been planning for years. Now it was front-page international news. Nobody expected the flight. Major Paul Barrows, Pearson Airfield commander, had his assistant commander, Lieutenant H.A. Reynolds, scurry to protect the airfield and post guards around the Soviet plane, wrangle mechanics and keep him informed for General Marshall.

The three-man Russian crew, thirty-three-year old Valery Chkalov, pilot; thirty-year-old Georgi Baidukov, copilot; and forty-year-old Alexander Belyakov, the navigator, were just getting their feet on the ground when Vancouver Barracks commander Brigadier General George Marshall's Packard came ripping down the airstrip to greet them. The future secretary of state's care of the Russian airmen was his first step into the nuanced world of international diplomacy, for which he'd win the Nobel Peace Prize in 1953.

The rainy day of the landing, Carolyn James was rushing her brother to the train depot. Driving by Vancouver Barracks, she stopped to gawk at a gigantic plane with "foreign writing." Back then, people didn't see aircraft with a 110-foot wingspan. She saw men climbing out of it wearing fur hats on their heads. James noticed that the propellors were still moving. She and her brother watched for about fifteen minutes and then headed for the train station.

Then ten years old, Larry Cassidy also remembered the landing. He never got close to the plane or the Russian fliers because military guards blocked him and the crowd of thousands, which gave the landing an air of secrecy and protected the ANT-25 from damage, which worried Chkalov.

The newly hired bartender Clyde Chmelik was wiping down the barracks bar about the same time as James and her brother stopped to see the great plane. Two of his buddies scurried in and demanded he come with them—the Russians had just landed. Chmelik met the fliers and shook their hands. One of the Soviet aviators passed him a chocolate bar, which he ate. Later, the foreign fliers enjoyed a beer at the barracks bar served by him.

The unexpected Soviets ate breakfast with General Marshall, post commander of Vancouver Barracks, before addressing crowds of journalists, politicians and inquisitive bystanders. Upon departing, they took a month-long tour of the United States, culminating in a reception with President Roosevelt in Washington, D.C.

According to Leverett Richards, a newspaper reporter covering the story who arrived an hour after the landing, Vancouver Chief of Police Harry Diamond wanted to "arrest them and take them downtown because they couldn't speak English" and were trespassing on government property. Fortunately, General Marshall intervened. Reporters wanted facts and interviews from the crew, pressing the general hard. He testily delt with the drove of reporters and photographers, forcing them back so the Russians could sleep. Richards waited in Marshall's library while the crew slept, anticipating the Soviet ambassador's arrival.

Ambassador Alexander Troyanovsky had been waiting in Oakland to greet the new Russian heroes and rushed from San Francisco to protect Soviet interests; help the aviators craft their narrative; and handle the crew's press conferences, military honors and public appearances. He made it to Vancouver by midafternoon their day of arrival, and the army greeted him with a nineteen-gun salute. When reporters grabbed him, he explained the Russians would be in America for about a month looking at aviation sites and planes, adding that the three men held the official title of "Hero of the Soviet Union."

Once Troyanovsky spoke with the fliers, the ambassador introduced them and Chkalov made a speech, saying something like the rivers of Russia and the rivers of America flow into the same ocean and we live on the same planet. We have a common planet—something like that. The next day, they were escorted downtown to the Padden Men's store, where the owner, James Padden, gave them their choice of hats. Tailors from Portland's Meier & Frank had already measured the crew for new suits.

The following day, General Marshall arranged for his guests to acquire business suits. Portland's Meier & Frank department store owner Aaron Meier Frank exchanged three new ones with them in trade for a fur-lined flying suit for his window display. However, the Russians declined to part with their long johns, which were made from silk and the most luxurious undergarments they'd ever known. The flying suits appeared in a Meier & Frank window display. Inside the suit pockets were found notes passed by the crew back and forth because it was too noisy to hear inside the ANT-25. The store management sought out a part-time clerk and teenaged Russian immigrant, Nadezhda Lenhart, to translate. Lenhart translated the notes and wrote down the gist of their content for herself. One of the notes poked fun, saying the copilot was getting sleepy. Eventually, one suit went to the Smithsonian, where it was tucked away. Much, much later, a curator pulled the misplaced suit out and, finding it full of bugs, tossed it away.

General Marshall hosted the crew and Ambassador Troyanovsky, relinquishing his family's breakfast of orange juice, eggs, bacon and coffee to his guests. Apparently, after breakfast, a bottle of the general's cognac disappeared, requiring its replenishment from other officers' homes on the post. Giving up their clothing, the three Soviets took a bath and a shave. As the crew bathed, one-hundred-dollar bills floated out a window and over the front yard of the Marshall house. They'd been given rolls of hundreds and left them on their dressers with the windows open, and the June breezes swept the money from their rooms, scattering the bills on the Marshalls' lawn.

Although the flight failed to break the long-distance record, it was the most dangerous ever taken. The world was headed to Vancouver, a town of fewer than eighteen thousand. International calls poured in. The Marshall home became clogged with newspeople. World leaders sent telegrams, including Joseph Stalin, President Roosevelt and Secretary of State Cordell Hull. The

Chkalov hands the black box to Major Paul Burrows, 31st Observation Squadron. Sent to Paris, it would certify the 5,288-mile nonstop transpolar flight. *Leverett G. Richards Collection.*

Vancouver Barracks and Portland feted the aviation heroes with parades and receptions in their honor.

The Soviet crew traveled the United States, first heading to San Francisco, where they met movie stars, then to the White House to meet President Franklin D. Roosevelt, before going to France and then home.

The ANT-25 wouldn't fly back to Moscow. Instead, the gigantic aircraft was disassembled in Vancouver by Danny Grecco under the watchful eye of a woman who recorded every part—each packaged and sent back to the U.S.S.R. The ANT-25 black box was presented to Major Paul Burrows, Pearson commander, by Chkalov. The box was sent to Paris to validate the transpolar flight. However, it eventually disappeared. Additionally, the War Department desired secret information about the aircraft's navigation equipment.

Navigator Alexander Belyakov worked as a professor at the Soviet Air Force Academy and died in 1983. Before his 1994 death, Baidukov wrote a book about Chkalov's life while serving in the Soviet Air Force until his 1988 retirement. He reached the rank of general colonel.

In December 1938, Valery Chkalov crashed while testing a prototype Polikarpov I-180, perishing in his plane just a year after the transpolar flight. While he could have bailed out, he chose to descend to his death, aiming his plane away from an apartment complex, where casualties would have been high. Although rumors circulated that Stalin orchestrated the crash, it was equally likely the crash resulted from Chkalov's independence and "well-known recklessness" combined with bad weather and engineers pressured to push the plane into early production to meet Stalin's five-year-plan goals.

Between Chkalov's polar flight and his death, several Soviet airplanes seemed to fall out of the sky and crash, including a second transpolar flight from Moscow to New York City piloted by Sigizmund Levanevsky. The N-209 disappeared over the North Pole. Neither the crew nor the plane were found. Such accidents, however, called into question Soviet pilots' proficiency and the quality of their aircraft.

Today, Russians remember Chkalov as the "Russian Lindbergh," recognizing his transpolar flight and other aviation achievements. His life became the subject for films, books and memorials. Lindbergh's celebrity was short and intense, while Chkalov's still endures in Russia yet is forgotten in the United States. In *Dictatorship of the Air*, Scott Palmer warns that Chkalov was only like Lindbergh to a point. Unlike Lindbergh, who represented American individualism, Chkalov could not be an independent "lone eagle" because of the risks of "overstating the importance accorded the individual by official Soviet culture." Chkalov's success was a three-man effort, fitting the ideal of a united effort for Communism, where his contribution didn't exceed that of the collective efforts of the crew. In Soviet aviation, it was this collective success that Stalin-era culture emphasized.

The transpolar landing in Vancouver secured Pearson Airfield's position in aviation history and left its mark on the city. Shortly, a small aviation community group wanted to celebrate Chkalov's accomplishment with a monument and even had a plaster of Paris model created, which was eventually lost. The first journalist at the landing, Leverett Richards, sent a letter to Stalin suggesting the establishment of a local Vancouver monument. It went unanswered. It would take a 1974 embarrassment to launch the project. A proposed monument built forty years late.

General George Marshall

In 1936, General George Marshall arrived at the Vancouver Barracks to command the Fifth Brigade and the Civilian Conservation Corps (CCC). A veteran of World War I, he handled the incident while commanding the Fifth, hosting the Soviet aviators in what is now known as the Marshall House. Few of General Marshall's biographers recognize his entry on the international stage started with the landing of the Soviet ANT-25 at Pearson field in 1937. Designed as a bomber, the Soviet ANT-25 landed unscheduled at Pearson Field and might have precipitated an international

General Marshall hosted the Soviet fliers after their unscheduled 1937 landing, providing clothes and lodging in addition to feeding them in his home and presiding over events honoring them. *Fort Vancouver Historical Site.*

incident at a time when U.S.-Soviet relations were fragilely forming. Marshall recognized the Russian flights had a darker side—the potential for bombing the United States. During World War II, he served as the Allies' senior military strategist. His handling of the landing, his gracious treatment of the Russian crew and his management of the CCC prepared General Marshall for rebuilding a weakened and devastated post–World War II Europe that Stalin eyed for expansion.

First U.S. Russian Monument: Chkalov 1937 Flight

When the Cold War ended in December 1991, few considered that its initial thawing started in Vancouver. In 1975, the world focused on the second coming of the surviving transpolar Russian fliers to dedicate a monument to their 1937 landing at Pearson Field. It almost didn't happen, despite a local reporter sending a never-answered letter to Stalin in 1937.

During the 1970s, a Russian immigrant's son, Peter Belov, helped Russian fishermen get medical assistance when they visited Portland. In 1974, he invited two Russian officers to see a typical American home in Vancouver. To his surprise, the foreigners knew the town's name and elatedly mentioned their comrades had landed here in 1937. The enthusiastic officers wanted to visit the landing site at Pearson Field and the monument erected there. Embarrassed, Belov explained no monument existed.

During the late 1930s, locals had talked of plans for honoring the fliers after the 1937 transpolar landing. News of the memorial plans even appeared in the Russian newspapers. And the Russian visitors remembered, even expected, a monument in Vancouver. But planning here was abandoned because the world was on the verge of a second world war.

A monument would come—even if thirty-eight years late. Belov and others were tenacious about that. First, Belov took his proposition to Columbia Machine Inc., where he worked translating technical documents into Russian. The company was receptive to his scheme, and soon the project was underway. Alexander Zinchuk, Russian counsel general in San Francisco, was also enthusiastic about the idea. He thought the plan significant because it began as a grassroots effort. Russian newspapers *Pravda* and *Izvestia* checked on the program's progress and often wrote about it.

Local folks showed little interest. The nation was riding out a recession. The lumber business was dying. Clark County faced a 15 percent unemployment rate. The winding down of the Vietnam War and Watergate

The Transpolar Flight Monument memorializing the historic 1937 flight stands today at Pearson Field. The Russians donated the brass plaque at the monument's center. *Wikipedia Contributors.*

In June 1975, Vancouver named Chkalov Drive after the Soviet pilot Valery Chkalov as part of the commemoration of the 1937 Soviet transpolar flight. *Clark County Historical Museum.*

ate at America's consciousness. News outlets were dubious about celebrating the Russians during the Cold War. A monument to Russian fliers wasn't on anyone's horizon. In the spring of 1975, the memorial was just a pile of sand, reported *The Columbian*. Still, Belov told everyone who'd listen it was a noteworthy symbol of détente and bounced around the Northwest, taking his message to businesses. Although he often irritated many, he convinced Richard Bowne, Clark County Public Utility District administrator, to get behind the movement. Bowne's slow, methodical manner balanced Belov's frenzied and exasperating approach. The two worked together undiscouraged by setbacks, forming a monument committee and collecting funds until they made the monument happen. While well-intended, Belov's technique was so chaotic, he nearly lost his committee role. Besides Columbia Machine, others were involved, including Allen Cole and Jess Frost.

In his travels, Belov explained that Soviet aviation wasn't merely transportation but an institution. The Soviet Union was so large that only aviation bound it together. Aviators were national heroes. After Chkalov's death, a Russian city bore his name. In school, children read about the transpolar flight. The transpolar crew members Chkalov, Baidukov and Beliakov were the seventh, eighth and ninth to be honored as Hero of the Soviet Union. The first six were also pilots. Americans have forgotten the transpolar flight, except in Vancouver.

The Chkalov Transpolar Flight monument was the first in the United States to memorialize a Soviet achievement. Initially, it stood on the north side of Washington State Route 14. When the route was widened in the 1980s, the memorial was relocated to its current site on the north side of Pearson Field on East Fifth Street between the Pearson Headquarters Building and the Air Museum.

After the 1975 dedication of what locals call the Chkalov Monument, the Vancouver hosts, Russian aviators and dignitaries dined overlooking the Columbia River at the Quay (the restaurant closed in 2015) before the Soviets traveled to San Francisco and Washington, D.C. According to a *Columbian* editorial, Vancouverites and the Soviet visitors "laid the basis for much friendship and understanding." Even Washington State Governor Dan Evans kept his talk unofficial and personal. When the 1937 copilot, General Georgi Baidukov, spoke, Irina Bastorini, the niece of Valery Chkalov, translated English into Russian for him. Discussions devoid of politics focused on "friendship between the nations and their peoples."

In the nation's capital, two Russian fliers, General Baidukov and General Alexander Belyakov, along with Chkalov's son, Colonel Igor Chkalov, appeared in full dress uniforms for the first time since arriving in the United States and met in the Rose Garden with President Gerald Ford. On the 1937 trip, the crew met President Roosevelt. President Ford recognized the Vancouver dedication of a Russian monument as "a fine example of a people-to-people meeting," adding, "It was good of the people of Vancouver to welcome the Soviet flyers with such warmth."

In 1987, the city commemorated the flight's fiftieth anniversary. Family members of the pilots visited Vancouver, and delegations of interested Vancouverites, including members of the Chkalov Cultural Exchange Committee, traveled to Moscow. The National Park Service commemorated the eightieth anniversary of the historic Soviet flight in 2017. The event featured a wreath-laying ceremony at the relocated monument.

6
BECOMING PEARSON FIELD

Between the 1920s and 1950s, Pearson Field's story involves two airstrips, one military and one commercial, coexisting. In the early days, the lines between the two were blurred at times. Each field had its own series of names. Each had its own dedication. After World War II, the army sold much of the field to Vancouver. Today the city owns and runs the airstrip, which buffers parts of the county from noisy overflights from Portland International Airport on the other side of the Columbia River.

Namesake: Alexander Pearson (1885–1924)

In 1917, Alexander Pearson enlisted in the Army Air Service and was commissioned after training at the San Francisco Presidio. When the Army refused to assign Pearson to the aviation branch of the Signal Corps, he resigned his commission in May 1917, only to reapply to re-test for flying the next month. Entering the service at Seattle, he was commissioned as a second lieutenant and served at Rockwell Field in San Diego.

Missing the action of the Great War, he stayed stateside as a flight instructor at several locations, including West Point, Illinois, Mississippi and Florida. When the war ended, he completed his studies at the University of Oregon. He became part of a small entourage of competitive fliers pushing the aviation boundaries of the day.

Eventually, he became one of the Air Service's more famous pilots by setting several distance and airspeed records. Then, in October 1919, he competed in the first transcontinental race billed as a sea-to-sea flight. He and his mechanic would be among fifty fliers leaving Roosevelt Field in New York and flying cross-country to Presidio's Crissy Field on San Francisco's Pacific coast. Another fifty fliers would take the reverse route to the Atlantic.

The race was limited to Army pilots flying De Havilland DH-4s. The pilots made stops at designated towns between Roosevelt and Chrissy Fields and then reversed their flight path, returning to their starting field. Pearson won by crossing the United States twice in forty hours, a world record, faster than his friend Lieutenant Oakley Kelly. He placed first, relying on a Rand McNally Railroad map to guide him across the country, winning a Thermos bottle, a leather flying suit and $825 in Liberty bonds. For his round trip between two oceans, he and the other competitors won the 1919 Mackay Trophy.

From June 1919 to November 1922, the Army assigned Pearson to the 12th Observation Squadron at Douglas, Arizona, flying reconnaissance along the U.S.-Mexican border with an eye out for bandits and rustlers and reporting back any he saw. While there, he decided he would fly from Florida to California, making a cross-country trip over the Southern states of the nation. His southern transcontinental route started at Pablo Beach, Florida, stopping in Houston, El Paso and then San Diego. He imagined the flight as a series of eight-hour jumps between each city and said he might finish the trip in less time by averaging ninety-five miles per hour. For the journey, he changed much of the De Havilland DH4-B, installing a new Lincoln Liberty

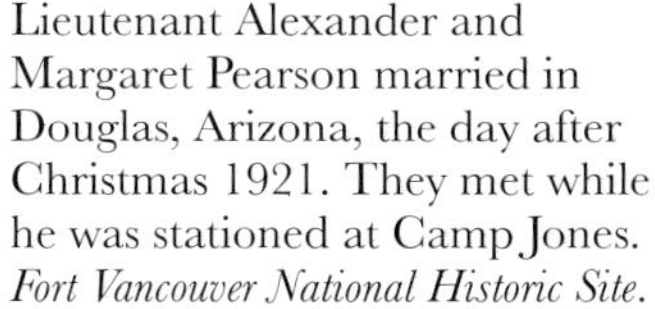

Lieutenant Alexander and Margaret Pearson married in Douglas, Arizona, the day after Christmas 1921. They met while he was stationed at Camp Jones. *Fort Vancouver National Historic Site.*

engine, moving the cockpit back to extend the fuel tanks and altering the oil, gas and cooling systems and finally the rigging and ignition for the long-distance trip. But first, he needed to fly the DH-4 to Pablo Beach.

He never made it.

Pearson soared from Douglas east toward Florida. By midmorning, the DH-4 De Havilland engine began failing a dozen miles east of Columbus, New Mexico, forcing him down. At his request, the Douglas base sent a second Liberty engine, so he swapped engines. The next day (February 8), he was off to Fort Bliss in El Paso, cruising at four thousand feet. The engine started vibrating. He scanned for a landing spot yet was too distant for communication and far from railroad tracks to follow.

Flying the De Havilland to over eight thousand feet, he tried circling in large spirals to descend. Listening to the engine noise, he hoped to regain oil pressure. Instead, after three hours of flight, the engine broke apart. It threw a rod, knocking out the bearings, jamming the crankshaft and forcing the plane to lose power.

Near the Rio Grande and needing smooth ground to land, he saw nothing but sand, cacti and mesquite below. Later he would claim he made the perfect landing in a small level area about five miles inside the Mexican border. When the plane was found, it was evident by its blown tire and broken wing that perfect didn't mean smooth. Trees slowed the aircraft's landing, acting as external brakes.

Not knowing where he landed, Pearson allowed the engine to cool so he'd have water to drink. Once he had water, Pearson left the crash site, wandering south for a day and a night, looking for any small settlement. The *Laredo Weekly Times* front page headline on February 13 screamed across three columns, "Army Aviator on Daring Flight Missing."

Newspapers across the country echoed that headline. While the search for Pearson was on, many fretted he was lost and dead. But not the Army, which sent sixty-five Army Air Service planes skyward along the border to find him. One, a giant Caproni photographic plane, was capable of picturing one hundred square miles at a time. Its pictures were enlarged and closely studied at San Antonio's Kelly Airfield. The Army ordered the planes to fly as close to the ground as possible. On February 10, planes dropped flyers asking if an aircraft had been seen.

At ground level, Army cavalry, cowboys and Texas Rangers scoured the area around Sanderson, Texas. Not finding the plane or the man after five days, everyone resigned themselves to the worst, and newspapers followed that. The Mexican government elevated the problem into a potential international crisis by articulating concerns about a U.S. pilot landing in Mexico.

At about 2:00 a.m. on February 11, Pearson smelled a skunk and heard frogs croaking, soon finding himself near the Rio Grande. He noticed the river flowing to his right, meaning he had landed in Mexico. A noose of anxiety surrounding the crash tightened around him. In 1919, a faulty airplane forced Army Lieutenants H.G. Peterson and P.H. Davis to land on the wrong side of the Mexican border. Desperados captured them, demanding a $15,000 ransom. The outlaws planned to take the money and kill the pilots. But Pearson knew the Army rescued them and would find him.

He formed a raft with the materials at hand. (Some say it was washtubs and others logs.) A broom handle and an old can were among the materials he formed a paddle with. Pearson floated down the river until he met two beaver trappers who shared food—bread, gravy and coffee—and he ate for the first time in three days. They said he was in Reagan Canyon in Big Bend country.

The three men rode burros to a candle wax factory and swapped them for horses. They stopped next at the Elder ranch and stayed a night. The next day, two of the rancher's boys escorted Pearson to Sanderson.

After being missing for five days, Pearson alerted the world that he was alive from Sanderson. First, he telegrammed his fiancée, Margaret Shannon, back in Douglas and then sent a second message to his parents in Portland, alerting them he was alive. Fortunately, his message to his fiancée reached her before the Army's statement about his loss and possible death. With typical optimistic bravado, he said he was in better shape after his desert trek than when he left on his flight east.

In May 1921, Pearson was ordered to survey the Grand Canyon. As a transcontinental flier, he was a good choice for exploring the area's geography for air service through the canyon. While conducting aerial photographic surveys of the canyon, he and his copilot, Sergeant Arthur Juengling, who held the Army rank of mechanic, flew into the deep abyss in June, becoming the first to do so.

As hundreds of onlookers watched, the men spent more than two hours in and alongside the Grand Canyon. At various depths in the canyon's throat, they fought to keep their plane aloft, struggling with temperature fluctuations and turbulence caused by heat swells. The only serious problem they faced was the engine overheating. Pearson also acknowledged he would have had difficulty without his copilot Juengling, who died in June the following year when his plane crashed into a mountainside.

His Mexican crash wasn't his last. Pearson, like many other famous early aviators, often pushed his aircraft and his skills to the point of failure. In 1922, a propellor malfunction caused Lieutenants Pearson and Paul Evans to crash two miles north of Fort Bliss. Then, when they were trying to land on a state highway, a car blocked them. So, they landed off the road. The plane dug in, crumpled its wings and cracked the motor. Later that year, a windstorm forced Pearson down west of El Paso, near Aston, New Mexico, damaging his plane. Then, flying in Waterville, Kansas, he crashed again.

In January 1923, as Orville Wright watched, Lieutenant Pearson and a civilian from McCook Field set a new air speed record—just short of 168 miles per hour—flying a Verville-Sperry R-39 propelled by a Wright motor. Before the year was out, he set two more speed records, 205 and 230 miles per hour. In September 1924, Pearson was practicing a dive for his second Pulitzer Race, flying in a Curtiss R-8. A strut broke, collapsing the wings. Enveloped in black smoke, the plane hit Wilbur Wright Field (now Wright Patterson Air Force Base) at 260 miles per hour, killing Pearson instantly. The crash was heard a mile away.

Investigating the accident, the Army discovered the cause—hollow, laminated struts that fluttered at high speeds. They replaced them with solid ones. But the crash also brought an order from the army—pilots must carry parachutes. The order may not have made test flying safer, but at least Army pilots might be mentally comforted with the possibility of jumping from a faulty airplane descending at high speed.

It was just a year later an airfield he never visited was named after the young airman: Pearson Airfield, Vancouver, Washington.

In *A Century Airborne*, Jon Walker offers a kind of postscript to Pearson's tragic death. John Wulle, one-time chairman of Pearson Air Museum, submitted a Freedom of Information request for particulars about Pearson's crash while preparing for his final race. Wulle received a "heavily redacted" report revealing little about the incident. It did note that the pilot was thrown outside the plane before it crashed and said the Army's Curtiss R-8 with a D-12 high-compression engine may have failed internally. An Air Force colonel explained the redaction was to prevent "embarrassing the witnesses or investigating officers." Those skeptical of the heavily blacked-out report might ponder why witnesses and investigators needed protection seven decades after the mishap, especially since by the time of Wulle's request, they were all likely dead.

Namesake Lacked Connection to Vancouver

Pearson Airfield was named after Alexander Pearson, a famous pilot who died in 1925. It was so named on the premise that Pearson had attended Vancouver High School. However, 2005 research by *The Columbian* found that the pilot never attended the local high school, and no airplane he piloted ever set down on the field bearing his name. Still, Pearson's parents, who had settled in Portland, supported honoring the airfield with his name.

In April 1925, with the Pearson family approval, Lieutenant Oakley Kelly petitioned the Army to rename the prewar polo grounds encampment area Pearson Airfield after Lieutenant Pearson, his friend and a renowned aviator who had crashed the previous September. He wanted a name with a stronger identity than Vancouver Barracks Aerodrome. Secretary of War Dwight F. Davis agreed and issued the order for the change.

Tradition had it that the dead pilot attended Vancouver High School, which was his connection with the area. This belief was often repeated, retold and republished. The source igniting the myth is a brief 1925 news article stating the field's namesake graduated from Vancouver High School.

Then in 2005, *Columbian* reporter Thomas Ryll, who was working on a story about Pearson's wife's scrapbook, dug deeper, debunking the long-held belief. When Ryll checked with the local high school, the administration told him they'd discovered no record of Pearson's attendance. Yet the myth was hardly squelched. Now we know he attended Hutchison High School in Kansas. As close as he got to Pearson Airfield was his family's move to Eugene, where he attended the University of Oregon. Later, his parents moved to Portland. Worse, there exists no aviation record showing any plane piloted by Pearson ever touching down or lifting off from the airfield. Regardless, the name stuck.

MANY AIR SHOWS AND TWO DEDICATIONS

Army's 1925 Dedication

Lieutenant Oakley Kelly finagled with the War Department and the Army to name the flying field, which was closed during World War I. During the war, only occasional planes scouting for forest fires flew during the Spruce

Cut-Up Mill days. Kelly came in with the 321st Squadron in 1923, assigned by the Army to turn a sizeable grassy polo area into an Army airfield.

The Army approved naming the airfield after Lieutenant Alexander Pearson, who had died a year earlier. As the first commander of the field, Kelly had hangars lifted; a runway graded; and storage sheds built for gas, parts and equipment.

The September 16, 1925 dedication followed just twenty years after the dirigible *Gelatine*, piloted by the eighteen-year-old Lincoln Beachey, touched down at what was the Vancouver Barracks Polo Field. In two decades, aviation at the field moved from bulky, slow-moving, lighter-than-air ships to speedy, svelte, heavier-than-air planes capable of flying seventy-five miles an hour or more. That year was also the one hundredth anniversary of the founding of Fort Vancouver. Today's restoration of the fort stands next to the Pearson Air Museum and the nearby airport.

When the War Department sanctioned the field's name, Kelly went to work planning the dedication. The day before the event, Kelly and five pilots of the 321st Squadron flew to San Diego's Rockwell Field to pick up planes and extend an invitation from the Vancouver Chamber of Commerce to that city's officials for the dedication. The day after, the fifty airplanes would zip east to Pendleton as guests of the Round-up Committee "with the privileges of the round-up at their disposal," said *The Columbian*.

Kelly sent telegrams to all the top fliers in the country, including John Macready, his partner in the first cross-country flight in 1923. Fliers from the Army's 1924 Transworld flight—Captain Lowell Smith and Lieutenants Erik Nelson and Leslie Arnold—were back visiting the field for the third time. Forty-five army planes and eight commercial planes attended. Some participated in the air circus, for which local merchants provided prizes. *The Columbian* reported the fliers would "display just about everything on the calendar of aerial navigation and stunt flying."

A crowd of twenty thousand gathered at the airfield and along the shore of the Columbia River for the dedication. A brief 1925 news article ignited a myth that the field's namesake, Lieutenant Alexander Pearson, graduated from Vancouver High School. (He graduated from a Kansas high school.) The dead lieutenant's parents and wife were at the field on dedication day from Portland.

The dedication event started at eleven o'clock, and all pilots flew over the field in a mob formation an hour and a half later. After landing, the pilots lunched, and a few officials gave short ceremonial speeches before the air circus started. Finally, a one-hundred-gun salute was fired to begin the day's events. Washington Governor Roland Hartley sent a message proclaiming that the "aviators taking part in today's ceremonies are pioneers in another great era of human achievement, and someday civilization will do them homage."

A microphone system and speakers were in place to keep the twenty thousand attendees updated on the day's events and to announce winners. (Some of the crowd spilled over to Oregon's Hayden Island Columbia Beach.) The speaker volume was boosted enough for those in the six thousand parked cars to hear. A presentation cup was given to the airfield sending the most significant number of planes. A second cup went to the field with the most flight hours. Other awards were given to the winners in each category.

Ace pilots competed in speed races, flew laps around the airfield, landed on mark, flew in competitive formations, raced relays, conducted stunts, dive bombed, demonstrated aerial combat, walked on wings and executed precision parachute landings. Besides Pearson fliers, pilots came from San Francisco's Crissy Field, San Antonio's Kelly Field, Sand Point Field near Seattle and Spokane Field. Captain Lowell Smith grabbed second and Lieutenant Kelly third in the De Havilland speed race, while Lieutenant A.B. McKenzie logged first in the Curtiss JN Jenny speed race. In the competitive formation contest, Sand Point won first place, pushing Pearson to second place and Spokane to third.

One event flooded the Portland telephone lines, for the callers believed a man fell to his death. So did many in the crowd who'd not heard the parachutist was a dummy and were screaming for him to open his chute. According to Walker, this wasn't a hoax or a joke. It had been intended to demonstrate the need for fliers to control a parachute. However, *The Oregonian*, which reported on the calls, remained unimpressed.

Five years later, the field was dedicated a second time for the opening of the municipal runway, featuring another air circus.

Air Dictionary

Preparing its readers for the Pearson Field dedication in September 1925, *The Columbian* published an "air dictionary" for landlubbers. Here are some of the terms the newspaper explained.

Flat spin—used to cast doubt on one's mental capacity
Pancake—a bad landing

Crate—description of disrespect for an aircraft
Crock—same as "crate" but more so
Flying brick—same as "crate" and "crock" but even more so
Streamline brick—another derogatory for an airplane
Dumb Bell—bum pilot
Lacks air brains—dumb pilot
Muscle bound between the ears—a poor pilot
The ceiling—an airplane's altitude limit
Mob formation—what will happen when 50-odd planes circle the airfield for the dedication on September 16

Louis Proctor Air Jubilee, 1929

In 1929, newspapers from Honolulu to Boston carried a nineteen-year-old Vancouver boy's name and face. The gangly teen had won first place in the National Airplane Model League of America contest. Weeks before, Louis Proctor placed second in a Tacoma, Washington "Lindy" model contest. Charles Lindbergh handed him the prize. Starting as a preteen, Louis Proctor built airplane models. Later, his national win granted him a six-week tour of Europe, where he met Louis Blériot and Orville Wright.

Proctor entered his first model airplane contest in 1926. Three years later, he built a Vought-Corsair model aircraft declared the best in the nation based on workmanship and design. The Vancouver boy beat out two hundred others for first place, garnering $200, a $100 gold cup, a medal and a trip to Europe. He traveled to Europe, all expenses paid, for six weeks with two other winners: Joseph Culver, indoor title holder, and Donald Burnham, holder of the world's outdoor record, a ten-and-a-half-minute flight.

As a teenager, Proctor hung around Pearson, earning a pilot's license, helping repair planes, working in the repair shop and learning the details he'd add to models. While the lanky teen with a big smile toured Europe and the nation showing off his model Vought-Corsair, the Vancouver Chamber of Commerce worked to promote the slowly emerging municipal airport. As a matter of civic pride, they sought commercial contracts and business for Vancouver.

Using Proctor's worldwide notoriety, the chamber raised money for the event and prizes. It grabbed an opportunity to publicize the field despite niggling legal issues surrounding leasing part of its land. Enthusiastic businesses downtown went so far as to create aviation displays in their windows.

The Vancouver Chamber of Commerce abandoned its original plan for a July 4 municipal airport dedication with an Army air show. Instead, it planned another featuring a Proctor air derby for its official opening, believing that mid-August and the Proctor show were timed better. By mid-August, the enlargement of the field, moving old hangars and building new ones would be finished. After six weeks in Europe, the triumphant youth would fly to Pearson Airfield to participate in the air derby. The local chamber even named the dedication event for the now-famous youth, the Louis Proctor Air Jubilee. After the jubilee, J.C. Penny's on Main Street displayed Proctor's winning model. A week after Proctor's air show, the boy spent his $200 national prize on an accordion.

The ad for the Jubilee linked the municipal airport and Pearson Field for the first time in print. It noted children under twelve and anyone carrying an airplane model attended free, while others paid fifty cents. Proctor would exhibit his award-winning model and judge a model-building contest. The commerce group also arranged for a unique postage imprint to commemorate the day. As usual for any air show, the Jubilee featured stunt flying, parachute jumping, balloon bursting, aerial relay races and wing walking. The Seventh Infantry forty-piece band from the Vancouver Barracks provided music all afternoon. On Jubilee Day, the Interstate Bridge set a crossing record of over eighteen thousand cars.

Louis Proctor built a non-flying Vought-Corsair model, winning first place in a national contest and an all-expenses paid tour of Europe. *Proctor Enterprises, Wilsonville, OR.*

In the end, the dedication of the field would not happen until 1930. The Louis Proctor Air Jubilee was a success, as was the Fourth of July Air Derby. Shortly after his air show, Proctor worked as a model builder for Boeing in Seattle and Ryan Aeronautics in San Diego. In 1964, he quit to create radio-controlled model kits of early aircraft with seven-foot wingspans. He eventually formed Proctor Enterprises Corp. The detailed models took customers three to four hundred hours to assemble. In 1982, Proctor sold his company and retired. But his models are so accurate that some were once used in a 1995 made-for-television movie, *Flight of the Hawkmen*. Today, Joe Topper is the company's third owner and sells Proctor's famous kits. Pearson Museum volunteers built two quarter-scale Proctor models for exhibit, a JN-4 Jenny and a Curtiss Pusher.

Municipal Airport Dedication, 1930

Forced labor helped build Vancouver's Municipal Airport during 1929. Several men guilty of vagrancy or drunkenness found themselves working at the nascent field constructing its first hangars while others cleared ground for more. Three prisoners took "French leave," as *The Columbian* chided. One was found dining downtown.

Even with forced labor, establishing a municipal flying field for Vancouver faced many barriers. The city leased part of the land from the railroad; sometimes, the field flooded, and the Army Air Corps 321st Squadron shared the space. Still, the city yearned for the status of an airport, motivated in part by an envy of Portland's new Swan Island Airport, which opened in 1927. So, the city was unwavering and resolved any problems, even seeking a bond issue in 1929. Although cheap labor helped erect the field's hangars, the town rented each for thirty dollars a month, and by March 1930, the city had rented the entire double row of them.

The rough municipal field saw modest use in the late 1920s. But by March 1930, it was in good shape and would open officially on May 25. An ad announcing the opening day featured a locomotive, an auto and a plane speeding past the winged Greek god Mercury. The text promised free general admission and parking for fifty cents. But the "penny a pound" airplane ride was a tease. The dollar minimum prevented children and the ultra-slim from flying too inexpensively. Below the ad's banner proclaiming "time, energy, distance," twenty advertisers anchored the event.

But the most significant change was the number of female contestants. The Army's 1925 dedication was all male. The City of Vancouver's dedication featured one woman, Edith Foltz, the number two finisher in the 1929 Powder Puff Derby. Foltz housed her plane in a Pearson hangar.

Edith Foltz poses with a group at the Vancouver Municipal Airport, perhaps at the 1930 dedication. Dubbed "Queen of the Airshow," she won the dead-stick landing. *Clark County Historical Museum.*

The Columbian called her a "noted aviatrix," stating she was among the few women holding a commercial license. The unbylined article described her as "small, slender and thin in smart flying togs with a colorful scarf about her hair, your Mrs. Foltz is the center of a lot of eyes." Unmistakably, the reporter was smitten.

Ten thousand attended the opening of the airport, some arriving at 8:00 a.m. Vehicles filled every available space for blocks around the field. Foltz, declared the queen of the show, won the dead-stick landing contest, collapsing the belief that a failed motor yields a crash, while showcasing a woman pilot's expertise. She halted her plane "almost squarely" on the finish line. (In a dead-stick landing, *dead* refers to the stopped engine and propeller while *stick* means the control stick. This means the pilot must glide onto the landing area.)

Other events included upside-down flying, Hap Roundtree performing stunts in an ordinary biplane and four glider flights. An auto towed the glider and pilot C.S. Murry until it lifted high enough for release. In the late afternoon, the audience heard speeches by Mayor John P. Kiggins and Judge George Simpson for the Elks. The judge raised the American flag before both speakers went aloft to drop a ceremonial wreath on the field. The day ended with the mayor's favorite pastime—a baseball game.

7
WOMEN CHALLENGE THE CLOUDS

After World War I, women also wanted the freedom of birds and sought out men who would teach them to fly. Often, they did. Silas Christofferson flew women over Vancouver; one of them, Edna Becker, married him but didn't become a pilot until after her husband died in a crash. A year before Charles Lindbergh soloed across the Atlantic, Tex Rankin ran a flying school at Pearson Airfield. Lindbergh's flight turned many to flying, filling Rankin's school. That year, Rankin signed up his first two women pilots, Faye Carter and Ann Bohrer. Regardless of their sex, as a good businessman, he wasn't going to turn anybody interested in flying lessons away.

Although neither became a commercial pilot, both flew for the joy of it. Their small stature earned them diminutive nicknames: Carter was "Tiny" and Bohrer "Half-Pint." With some exaggeration, Bohrer's brother, Walt, writing in *America's Famous Fliers—A Pictorial History: Tex Rankin* says Carter and his sister sat on "five pillows in order to see out of the cockpit." Both were likely the first women to parachute in the Pacific Northwest, something Rankin required of all his pilots.

Carter's student pilot card, permit 298, cites December 16, 1927, for her solo flight. It also notes she was just under five feet and weighed 110 pounds, with brown hair and brown eyes. She gained notoriety as a pilot and parachutist for a few years but disappeared from aviation history and could not be found by *Oregonian* journalist Leverett Richards when he wrote a story about the early days of aviation for the newspaper.

An early pilot, Faye Carter, stands by Tex Rankin's *Queen of the Cascades*. Oddly, she stopped piloting and couldn't be found for a later reunion. *Oregon Historical Society.*

Native American Competitor: Mary Riddle (1902–1981)

Perhaps because she was named after a bird, she took to flight naturally. Her grandmother gave her the Quinault name Kus-de-cha, meaning "kingfisher." A kingfisher not only flies but also swoops down to catch fish. Once Mary Riddle learned to fly, she became the most famous female parachutist in the West and swooped to earth, capturing audience attention like a kingfisher catches a fingerling.

Marie Agnes Riddle, known as Mary Riddle, was the daughter of Albert "Doc" Riddle (1874–1912), who belonged to the Quinault tribe. Her mother, Elizabeth Bob (1881–1905), was a Clatsop. Although not much is documented about their daughter, she was the first Native American woman to fly and obtain a pilot's license. While no records state this, she was likely also the first to make a parachute jump.

Shown here about 1930, Mary Riddle was called the "parachuting stewardess" when traveling the West in the *Voice of Washington* plane. *Oregon Historical Society.*

In 1927, Riddle paid for her first flight in Aberdeen, Washington. Afterward, she wrote to Tex Rankin's school, asked about her chances of flying, and saved money for two years before enrolling.

Rankin taught her to fly about 1929, and she soloed in 1930. "I wasn't scared," Riddle said. "I just missed the weight of the instructor in the plane." She received a pilot's license a little later. As part of training his pilots, Rankin insisted they parachute from an airplane. Riddle later put jumping out of planes to profitable use.

Once trained, she spent weeks practicing her part of an air circus performing at the 1930 Rose Festival. Then, dressed in traditional Quinault costume, she rode a horse up to her plane, dismounted, climbed into the cockpit and took to the sky. Later, she frequently flew wearing her Native costume, even being featured on a Ninety-Nines' magazine cover in it.

After obtaining her license, Riddle went barnstorming around the country with a group from Seattle. At that time, airports were few, and most were under development. New airports frequently sponsored air shows as part of their opening ceremonies. Sometimes they became regular events intended to increase their air traffic. Riddle made over forty parachute exhibition jumps at airports around the Northwest and at least as far east as Bismarck, South Dakota. She later claimed that she had visited almost every state in the Union barnstorming with the Seattle air circus.

Knowing that women parachutists were always a big draw, Riddle applied under her Quinault name to the Spartan School for parachutists in Tulsa, Oklahoma. The school accepted her application. However, administrators turned her away when she arrived because the school didn't train women. After two weeks of lobbying, she became the first woman to attend and the only one in her class. In Tulsa, Riddle studied advanced flying techniques and navigation. Still, prejudice persisted. No male pilot would consent to take her aloft to parachute. Then she met a man who wanted to open an airfield and was looking for a woman parachutist.

In 1937, Riddle joined the crew of the *Voice of Washington*, reputedly the largest plane Boeing manufactured at the time. The aircraft was part of a promotion of both Washington State and Boeing. The plan was to fly the trimotored plane around the state, stopping here and there to highlight industrial opportunities and the scenic beauty Washington offered. First, the team planned to fly to Arlington, Washington, and then to the most northwesterly airport in the country, Port Angeles, and finally south to Olympia, where the governor would dedicate the flight. After that, it was on to Montana and the Dakotas.

The crew included a pilot, copilot, two flight attendants (Riddle was one), an advertising agent, a ticket seller and a mechanic. At that time, flight attendants were often public relations personnel at airports, giving tours of planes and airport facilities. Riddle was the only parachuting stewardess. The Boeing plane cost seventy-five dollars an hour to operate, including fuel and crew salaries.

At Arlington, the crew kept Mayor Henry Backstrom waiting. They arrived twenty-three hours late, thanks to an unplanned government inspection. Despite *The Voice of Washington*'s day-late arrival, the Arlington airport overflowed with aviation enthusiasts. Riddle stepped out and saluted the crowd. Wearing their finest Native costumes, Tulalip Chief Shelton and a dozen members of the tribe greeted her and posed for photos as the rest of the crew descended from the plane. Immediately, the ticket seller hawked tickets for flights aboard the plane.

Advertisements for the Bismarck parachute jump billed Riddle as both stewardess and parachutist. A photo story in the *Bismarck Tribune* noted her as charming, quiet and with humility belying her "unusual courage and daring." The parachuting stewardess made her jump in Bismarck from the trimotored aircraft as advertised. She made her last parachute jump in 1938. Throughout the 1930s, Riddle often showed off her athletic skills at other daring feats, including swimming and performing motorcycle stunts.

Being one of the few women in the country with a commercial license made her an asset when World War II broke out. The War Department recruited her for an Army engineering school, where she learned how to inspect military airplanes. Afterward, the department sent Riddle around the country to check out planes before pilots flew them. She also worked as a sheet metalworker at the Malden Army Airfield in Idaho.

In 1975, Riddle was working as a receptionist for Gibbs and Hill, an engineering consulting service. In a phone interview, an *Oregonian* reporter spoke with her. Riddle said she was still flying and had a transport license but refused to give her age. "Age makes no difference....I still have my license... and I flew the last time to Seattle," she said.

WAR HERO: EDITH FOLTZ (1902–1956)

When America entered the Second World War, male pilots were at a premium. Jacqueline Cochran, an able pilot and self-promoter, whispered into First Lady Eleanor Roosevelt's ear about using women to make up the difference. She also lobbied Major General Henry "Hap" Arnold of the Army Air Corps. After the Battle of Britain, the depletion of the British aviator ranks caused England to create a ferry service using women, but they couldn't fill its ranks fast enough. Arnold gave Cochran approval to recruit women pilots from the United States.

Perhaps selling tickets for a flight, Edith Foltz models her patented Foltz-up designed for women pilots going from the cockpit to dinner. *Oregon Historical Society.*

There were 444 U.S. women pilots in 1937. The number likely grew slightly by World War II. This small group had the core experience Cochran sought for the British Air Transport Auxiliary (ATA) recruitment. She mailed letters and recruited 27 women pilots. Two of those letters went to women pilots who often flew out of Pearson Field: Evelyn Burleson Waldren and Edith Foltz. Burleson turned the opportunity down, saying she had to care for her mother. Foltz, who wasn't much of a homebody and was always looking for a place in the sky, grabbed the chance to ferry planes and traveled from Montreal, Canada, to England to fly with the ATA and contribute to the war effort.

After graduating from Dallas High School, Edith Margalis studied music, piano and voice at Lenox Hall, hoping to become a singer. In 1946, Leverett Richards wrote in *The Oregonian* that she had a promising singing career. But after a move to Oregon, she married Joseph Foltz Jr., a former World War I aviator and celery baron. They had children, Richard Joseph, born in 1924, and unnamed premature twins, who died from respiratory failure thirty-six hours after birth in 1922. Joe ran a small barnstorming operation from Swan Island. At the time, Swan Island had no hangars, so aviators had to tie their planes down to stop winds from blowing them away.

Edith began selling tickets at barnstorming events for her husband, who encouraged her to get flight instruction. After less than two hours of training, she soloed in 1928. Her first landing attempt overshot the runway. Her second undershot it. The third was almost perfect. During a postwar interview with *Oregonian* reporter Leverett Richards, Foltz recalled being so relieved after her solo that she released the controls too quickly and spun in a loop on the ground. "I never did that again," she laughed. Orville Wright signed her pilot's license. She bought an airplane that year, eventually making a name for herself as a barnstormer during an era when women were expected to pilot kitchen stoves and not airplanes.

Foltz entered the first Women's Air Derby in 1929, placing second in the light aircraft division. Aviation enthusiast and humorist Will Rogers dubbed the race the "Powder Puff Derby" during the radio broadcasts that followed the race from Santa Monica, California, to Cleveland, Ohio. He added that "the stronger sex went back to the kitchen sink and the radio."

Nineteen fliers lifted off from the Santa Monica runway, competing for $8,000 in overall prize money. Among the women joining Foltz in the women's first cross-country race were Amelia Earhart, Marvel Crosson, Pancho Barnes, Louise Thaden and Blanche Noyes—all noted pilots and a few even record holders. The fliers had no instruments, radar or control towers, but the flight path was carefully planned, with daily stops at designated towns for rest and food. The pilots carried roadmaps detailing the major roads and railways along the route to plot their way.

Most of the women piloted open-cockpit biplanes, making hanging on to maps tricky. Foltz was the exception. She flew a new Alexander Eaglerock Bullet, one of the few monoplanes in the race and among the first with an enclosed cabin, leaving her little worry about maps fluttering away. Foltz started the race confidently, knowing her new Eaglerock Bullet, a low-wing monoplane, was among the fastest. It was an airplane many men didn't think a woman could handle. Reporter Leverett Richards described it as "tricky as a Balkan politician."

When a few of the women discovered unusual damage to their planes, Foltz believed they were sabotaged. She claimed a fire in Blanche Noyes's plane looked odd to her. She questioned a broken strut on Claire Fahy's ship as equally bizarre, claiming that struts don't break on maintained airplanes. Edith added that it wasn't the women one had to look out for but the men. Regardless, race officials blamed the women for the mishaps, pointing out hasty or improper servicing as the cause. One Kinner Service Expert told the press, "The girls become nervous and excited. Most of them know very little about the planes they fly. They take the word of airport mechanics that everything is all right." It occurred to no one that the local men making, inspecting and repairing the race planes weren't sufficiently thorough. Interestingly, Foltz made a similar comment about women fliers in 1936. "The trouble with women as aviators is that they don't like to get their hands greasy—cleaning sparkplugs and the like," she said.

On Monday, August 29, at the race's end, only fifteen fliers reached Cleveland. On her last leg of the derby, a misdirection near Cleveland led to some official consternation and scrutiny but yielded Foltz a hot meal. Feeling unwell, Foltz wasn't locating the Cleveland airport. She spotted and swooped a small field. Deciding it was too tiny for the race's end, she flew on. Flying thirty minutes more, she finally landed in a farmer's field, taxiing to his front door. He, of course, was startled, likely never having seen a plane before, certainly not one in his front yard. He explained Foltz had passed Cleveland and offered her a chicken dinner. She accepted, enjoying the meal and returning to the Cleveland airport after. Her detour befuddled the race officials. Then, checking her story out, they awarded her second place behind Phoebe Omlie but ahead of Jessie Keith-Miller, third, and Thea Rasche, fourth.

Although the iconic female aviator Amelia Earhart was in the heavy plane category, finishing third, Foltz's time was better. Nearly every year through the mid-1930s, the Oregon aviator participated in derbies and air shows, continuing racing into the 1950s. When interviewed by the Vancouver paper a few days before the air show, Foltz said she would fly her Eaglerock to "demonstrate that there is nothing a modern girl can't do."

As the only woman competitor in the 1930 dedication of Pearson's Municipal Airport, the "queen of the air show" shamed the men when her dead-stick landing stopped her black and orange plane just feet from the mark. Two years later in a Cleveland air show, she came in second in the dead-stick landing. By October, she had a job copiloting charters for West Coast Air Transport, making her the fifth woman to earn a commercial pilot's license and the first to fly a trimotor commercial aircraft.

In 1929, Foltz became a founding member of the Ninety-Nines, the first professional organization for women pilots, and held positions within the organization. However, she failed to launch a Northwest chapter because the pilots lived too far from one another. Foltz, aerobatic champion Dorothy Hester Stenzel and Edna Christofferson, wife of daredevil Silas Christofferson and a pilot, co-founded the Women's National Aeronautic Association branch in Portland in 1930.

That year, when interviewed by *The Columbian* for the dedication of the Municipal Field, Foltz told the reporter her flying career started with barnstorming. "We would land somewhere, and I would sell the tickets for airplane rides to local people," she explained to reporters. "Then I finally got the idea that I might possibly become a licensed pilot."

Foltz's experience racing in the 1929 Women's Derby inspired her to design a versatile outfit for women fliers. She designed and patented the Foltz-up, an outfit that made it easy to go directly from the cockpit to dinner. Wearing the Foltz-up, women pilots could pull a couple of zippers, transforming them out of a pilot wearing a jodhpur-like flight pants look and switching to an attractive dress ready for an evening out. During the 1930s, Portland retailer Meier & Frank sold copies of her patented dress.

Foltz continued participating in air shows during the early 1930s, including one in Chehalis, Washington, in July 1931. On July 5, the day of the air circus, Foltz and Gladys O'Donnell, who placed in the Power Puff Derby heavy division, were among the fifty fliers showing off their skill. Before the Second World War, she divorced Joseph Foltz and married her second husband, Harry Stearns. After the marriage, she went by the surname Foltz-Stearns. Together they started Oregon Airways, and she taught flying at the Multnomah Flying Club. They suspended the airline during World War II.

Under wartime restraints, Jacquline "Jackie" Cochran's recruitment of American women pilots for the Air Transport Auxiliary (ATA) was done secretly. No one was supposed to know. Unfortunately, a photo of one leaked out and appeared in an Orange County, New Jersey newspaper. Locally, Larry Gilbertson, *Oregon Journal* aviation editor, saw it and tracked down Foltz to do a story on the local aviator joining the war in England. Cochran was furious. She'd ordered the pilots not to speak to the press, making them adhere to wartime restrictions. She sent letters to both Foltz and Gilbertson.

In an undated letter to Foltz, Cochran wrote:

> *I am more distressed than I can say about this, because as I stressed both to you and Miss Burleson, it is imperative that we have no publicity released by any of you girls. I wonder how they got hold of this information.…I hope that we can find a way that the* [Oregon] Journal *will not publish anything, and I am going to leave it to your good judgment to see that it is handled.*

But Cochran knew she had to balance her anger and could not lose any fliers, so she concluded pleasantly, "Looking forward to seeing you, and with kindest personal regards." When recruited, Foltz had fourteen years of piloting experience and two thousand flight hours.

Despite telling Foltz to kill the story, Cochran sent Gilbertson a rather political epistle, saying she lacked authorization from either the Americans or British for any story because her pilots were not to be publicly identified due to war restrictions. She explained that the Orange County, New Jersey leak was beyond her control. She ended the letter by relaying that wartime restrictions prevented her from giving a "green light" for a story on Edith Foltz.

The U.S. government took care of getting the fliers' visas, but weather conditions delayed their departure for several weeks. Luggage was limited to two hundred pounds. The fliers knew any carry-ons might put them overweight. Although Flight Captain Cochran traveled to England and did some ATA training and even flew a bomber there, the first woman to do so, General Arnold called her back to organize a similar group, the Women's Flying Training Detachment (WFTD), to train civilian women pilots to free American men for air combat. Soon after, the WFTD merged with Nancy Love's Women's Auxiliary Ferrying Squadron to form the civilian Women Airforce Service Pilots (WASPs), which Cochran led from 1943 to 1944.

Foltz entered the ATA as a cadet in 1942, traveling there with her son, Richard. She held a T-officer rank (flight leader equal to a captain) when she left in 1945. Flying for the ATA during her ferrying career, Foltz found herself in the cockpit of fifty different aircraft, including fighters, transports

Edith Foltz Stearns flew for ATA during World War II in England for 1942 to 1945. She is pictured here in her ATA uniform at the end of the war. *Public domain.*

and bombers. It was a tough job flying without a radio or a navigator in a new aircraft every day.

Initially, the ATA women could fly only single-engine airplanes, but they did so well that soon they were flying dual-engine bombers. Other ATA pilots, like Foltz, flew a wider variety of aircraft than the male pilots did because they ferried planes back and forth to where they were needed or returned them to England for repairs. The women flew planes from factories in England to the combat areas. On the return, the aircraft they piloted often were damaged or needed repairs and carried no ammunition. If German pilots spotted an unarmed woman pilot, their only choice was outflying, outmaneuvering, outrunning or hiding themselves in the clouds from the enemy.

In a 1945 interview with the *Salem Statesman Journal*, Foltz related how she was nearly a victim of friendly fire. Flying into the south of England in a pursuit plane, she recalled how she was mistaken for a Nazi buzzbomb. As Ack Ack antiaircraft shells burst around her, she admitted to being "plumb scared." For a moment she thought about dropping her wheels to show she was a friendly. But the Ack Ack continued, so Foltz throttled the pursuit and got away as fast as possible. In a 1947 article, she explained that although the ATA pilots flew unarmed, she was shot at several times because the Germans couldn't tell the difference between armed and unarmed planes.

Foltz's solo ground loop wasn't her only airplane mishap. She was sanctioned for hitting another plane in the ATA. While preparing a Defiant interceptor for takeoff, she crept ahead and struck a Magister, as noted in her ATA record. The unit also suspended her for a week for "willful neglect of duty of an ATA pilot" and for misuse of a transport. Still, after her two years ferrying for the ATA, Foltz received the King's Medal for the Cause of Freedom, the highest commendation awarded by the British to foreigners who provided exceptional contributions in furthering the interests of the British Commonwealth. Foltz explained why she stayed with the ATA rather than returning home and joining the WASPs. "The British treated us strictly as pilots, according to our experience and ability without regard to sex," she told *Oregonian* reporter Leverett Richards in 1946.

After the war, she returned to Portland and sold real estate for a while. Always trying to find ways to fly, she moved to Texas. There she married her third husband, a rancher named Grissom, of whom little is known. A 1947 Corpus Christi article on her cited her as Edith Foltz Stearns Grissom and noted she married a third time on April 26 that year. The article announced Foltz's decision to get back into aviation and said she was instructing at the Irwin School of Flight at Cuddihy Field (now Cuddihy Field Airport).

In 1952, Cuddihy Field sponsored Foltz and Pauline Gleason, also a flight instructor, to fly in a transcontinental air race. Two years later, when Foltz entered a derby from Long Beach, California, to Knoxville, Tennessee, race officials disqualified her because she entered a Cessna 180 but changed to a Cessna 140. She flew anyway, saying her sponsor Jay Callahan wanted the flight for her because it was her "silver anniversary in air racing."

Before her death, Foltz was the primary instructor training naval cadets on instrument flying using a Link (flight simulator) at Corpus Christi. She was also a member of the local Ninety-Nines unit that was painting the roofs of towns to prevent pilots from getting lost. A cancer diagnosis led to her early death in 1956. Her age at death is uncertain. Different sources claim she was born in 1900, 1902 or 1903. Upon her death, the *New York Times* incorrectly reported that Foltz won the 1927 Powder Puff Derby. The first women's derby was in 1929, and she finished second. During her life, Foltz flew hundreds of different aircraft, logging more than five thousand flight hours.

Bursting Social Barriers: Leah Hing (1907–2001)

Even before she took flight, Portland-born Leah Hing sought out adventure and broke down gender and racial barriers. She played basketball, played the saxophone on the vaudeville circuit and was among the first Chinese women to operate an elevator in color-conscious Portland. Even after many proposals, the determined Hing announced she'd never marry and give up her independence.

Hing's family was prominent in Portland's Chinese community and endured the anti-Asian sentiment of the early twentieth century. Her grandfather came to this country from China. Although born in Portland, her father had to prove his citizenship in a local court. Interestingly, her parents took on a month-old Caucasian foster child, George Lee Reynolds. This was a rare instance, especially in racially biased communities like Portland.

Hing, a graduate of Washington High School, had broad interests, and news stories about her could be found in society, sports and news pages of *The Oregonian* starting about 1923. As a sixteen-year-old member of a Baptist Chinese mission organization called the Tanda group, she and other girls received training about symbolism and its relation to the Chinese ceremonial gown. She and some of the group danced in *Rosaria*, the final performance for the Rose Festival of 1927. The girls wore embroidered Chinese costumes with tassels and garlands in their hair as they danced. Hing was the president of the club.

About 1928, she and a few friends decided to start an all-Chinese girl orchestra. The girls raised money to buy instruments to form the band. With the funds raised, they purchased several instruments—two saxophones, a trombone, cymbals, a drum and a xylophone. One of the friends already played the banjo, and they added that to the eclectic group of instruments. Except for the banjo player, none of the orchestra members had experience with musical instruments.

They trained for a year with ex-vaudevillian Chuck Whitehead, then director of Dufwin's Orchestra in Portland. In May 1928, they played at a Mother's Day tea at an eatery her father was part owner of, the Hung Far Low restaurant. Hing played the saxophone.

The group performed well enough to sign a two-year contract with the Radio-Keith-Orpheum vaudeville circuit as members of Honorable Wu's Vaudeville Troup. The orchestra traveled first to New York and then around the country. On the tour, the band lived hand-to-mouth but traveled the nation, at a time when few Chinese found work outside a laundry or restaurant.

A 2001 *Oregonian* story quotes Hing admitting the group didn't take many lessons and the band could play only one song, "Happy Days Are Here Again." Across the country, they played that song, even for encores. Today, it seems odd that Chinese girls in embroidered costumes played an American song on European instruments. But during the 1920s, it was ordinary. When the band folded, its members returned to Portland.

After the band's demise, Tex Rankin, who often dined at the Hung Far Low restaurant on Northwest Fourth Avenue in Portland, met Hing and suggested she take up flying. He'd already trained Mary Riddle to fly and do stunts—why not a Chinese woman? Rankin could see promotional opportunities in this. The adventuresome Hing told him she'd give it a try. By then, she'd already experienced her first ride in an airplane in Chicago during her vaudeville tour.

Flying with Rankin, she did well. The day after her first fifteen-minute lesson, *The Oregonian* published a story titled "Chinese Girl Flying Pupil Quick to Acquire Knack" with a photo of Rankin shaking hands with Hing, dressed in a leather helmet and flight jacket. In that first lesson, she was already coordinating all the controls of the training plane, and she landed the plane with little help from Rankin.

During that flight, Rankin taught Hing how to move the rudder to the extreme right and left positions. He showed her how to use ailerons to lift and lower the craft and how to use elevators to dive and zoom the ship several times. She did all these maneuvers after just ten minutes of instruction. Rankin's remark about this feat: "That's unusual for the first time for anyone."

Rankin often made his students solo at Pearson Field because of its size. Hing recalled in her oral history that she was scared on her first solo. Rankin's and his instructors' habit was not to warn the student but to exit the craft and say, "All right, take it around." She laughed when the interviewer asked about navigation, saying she followed "railroad tracks." Hing also played for and managed the Chung Wah basketball team for at least two years while training with Rankin.

Rankin taught Hing to fly when flying consisted of a few lessons and then a solo. Soloing amounted to taking off, circling an airfield and landing without incident. But flying involved more competent navigation, coping with wind and foul weather, dealing with mechanical problems and anything unexpected. After her solo flight, Rankin declared Hing a natural.

There has been confusion about which Chinese woman received her pilot's license first. Leah Hing was the first Chinese woman to fly and land an airplane and hoped to be the first to earn a pilot's license. Instead, she took third place. By the time she'd secured her license in 1934, the China-born Katherine Sui Fun Cheung (1904–2003) had earned the title of "first licensed" Chinese woman. Cheung obtained her license in Los Angeles on March 29, 1932. Hazel Ying Lee (1912–1944) of Portland, Oregon, was awarded a pilot's license in October that year, making her the second. However, Ying might be the first Chinese woman to fly a military plane because she was in the WASPs.

Hing joined the Ninety-Nines, the all-woman pilot organization founded by ninety-nine licensed female pilots after the 1929 Powder Puff Derby. In 1941, she became the secretary-treasurer of the newly reorganized Oregon chapter.

When Japan invaded China in 1931, Hing, Cheung and Lee felt outraged and longed to help their ancestral country. Cheung raised $7,000 and purchased a Ryan ST-A. She hoped to fly to China to train pilots. However, a prankster crashed her plane and grounded her effort. The Portland Chinese Benevolent association was collecting money to buy planes to train Chinese pilots at Pearson Airfield. Hing also dreamed of going to help China. She didn't go for a common Chinese cultural reason—her father, Lee Hing, told his independent daughter no.

To soften the blow, he let her buy a Fleet Model 7 biplane for $1,000. Hing flew in a few West Coast air shows. But she enjoyed her surprise fly-ins to see friends more. To see her brother, Peter, and his wife, Gertrude, she flew to Aurora, Oregon, easily landing her plane in a wheat field.

Her landings weren't always so perfect. The Fleet Model 7 might have been jinxed. She flipped it when she hit a hole hidden by weeds in a landing zone but had it rebuilt. She also crashed it at Boeing Field near Seattle in September 1937. Once, her aircraft was hit while idle on the ground. She wasn't even near it. Hing's biplane was parked when a much larger Stearman biplane landed, taxied over to the fueling area, slammed into the Fleet and "chopped it up like so much kindling," wrote Levertt Richards in 1981.

She was lucky, nonetheless. The State of Washington owned the Stearman. Its pilots were Lacey and Edward R. Murrow. Edward would become famous for his on-the-scene radio broadcasts during the London Blitz and later as a television broadcaster in the 1950s. Doing the right thing, the embarrassed brothers bought her plane. With the money, she purchased Dorothy Hester's Travel Air. (Rankin also trained Hester, who became a champion aerobatics pilot and held records for the most outside loops and snap rolls.) The Murrow brothers repaired the jinxed aircraft and sold it. The plane, number N794V, seemingly disappeared into obscurity, and Hing lost track of it.

With the build-up to World War II, the Army encouraged the federal government to begin training civilian pilots under a civil air program. Many airfields and college campuses began teaching pilots. The ratio of students was one woman for every ten men. Some women trained in this program entered the Women's Air Service Program. Others, like Hing, became members of the Civil Air Patrol.

After the bombing of Pearl Harbor, the civilian training program became the Civil Air Patrol. The war grounded most internal flights. This put a crimp in Hing's flying, so she joined the Civil Air Patrol and did some reconnaissance flying. Hing said she drilled on the ground more than she flew during her Civil Air Patrol service. She also worked as an airplane instrument technician. An *Oregonian* photo essay in May 1942 shows two pictures of her. One depicts her working on an airplane instrument. A second shows her wearing a parachute and sliding half inside the cockpit of a P-38 Pursuit plane WASPs piloted from manufacturers to military air stations—a plane she would never fly.

The war also brought the internment of the Japanese. At a time when being mistaken for Japanese could cost one's life, the Chinese societies took precautions to help the public sort out the two Asian populations. To distinguish the friendly Chinese from the Japanese enemy, the Portland Chinese societies passed out buttons with pictures and words identifying the wearer as Chinese. Hing remembered wearing one. She also recalled she and other Chinese were told to carry unique identification cards listing their personal information.

After the war, Hing discontinued her flying career, letting her pilot's license expire in 1947. In 1936, she broke another barrier and became the hat check girl and elevator operator for Portland's exclusive Aero Club. As a Chinese American, she was unable to join the club, a private social club for pilots and aviation enthusiasts. So, she worked there as a "hat check girl," switchboard operator, photographer and receptionist until her retirement in 1971 at the age of seventy. Years later, she would joke that she was the only licensed pilot there. After letting her license lapse, she said she wasn't afraid to travel and "enjoyed flying as a passenger."

In August 1991, Hing's jinxed N974V turned up. It had flown a twisted path. T.V. Ridgway, a Portland collector of antique automobiles and aircraft, called her. In May, he'd bought the plane from the man who restored it, John Hart. Hart hangared the plane at Evergreen Airport in Vancouver. At that year's annual Evergreen Airport fly-in and Antique Air Show, Hing climbed aboard the plane and settled into the familiar cockpit.

The legacy of Leah Hing, who died in 2001 at ninety-three, lives on in the Portland-Vancouver area. Portland artist Alex Chiu painted Leah Hing in a mural near the corner of Fifth and Main Streets in Vancouver to celebrate her training at Pearson Airfield, her personal independence and her barrier-breaking aviation success as a minority woman pilot.

As an endless promoter of aviation, Rankin recognized that aircraft were indifferent to who sat in the pilot's seat. "It's as much a woman's game as a man's game," he said. "Aviation will never be a great industry until women come on par with men." At one time, he claimed to have sixty-five women students. Although probably out of self-interest, he did contribute to the slow leak that let women into aviation. Still, despite American women piloting military planes as WASPs and for the ATA, it would be more than fifty years—1993—before a woman achieved Air Force fighter pilot status.

Throughout her life, Hing stayed engaged in Portland's Chinese community, coaching girls' basketball, donating money for the elderly and assisting newcomers with the naturalization process. She considered herself a rebel of sorts, who enjoyed demanding activities.

Leah Hing's Airplane Returns

The snazzy orange 1931 Fleet Model 7 that ninety years earlier Hing had sailed through Northwest skies found its way to Pearson Air Museum. Since 2022, it's been on permanent display at the museum. Aviation enthusiasts and curious visitors can view her Fleet 7 there during normal visitors' hours free of charge. The move was brought about by a partnership between the

Leah Hing reunited with her 1931 biplane, once destroyed, at Evergreen Airport in 1990. Today the plane is on display at the Pearson Museum. *From* The Columbian.

Fort Vancouver National Historic Site and The Historic Trust. Hing trained with Tex Rankin at Pearson Field. She also trained with Pat Reynolds, of the 321st Squadron, received her pilot's license in 1934 and joined the Ninety-Nines in 1939, serving as secretary-treasurer in 1941. Denied by her father to fight the Japanese in China, she worked with the West Coast Civil Air Patrol in World War II.

Leah Hing's plane is today in a permanent home near where she learned flying from Tex Rankin and not far from where she first soloed. Her story is an important one for Asian women and a treasured piece of Pearson history. Her story is how one minority woman broke barriers in society and aviation.

ADVENTURER AND DEADEYE: EDNA CHRISTOFFERSON (1886–1945)

Edna Christofferson watched her daredevil husband, Silas, fly off the Multnomah Hotel headed for the Vancouver Barracks polo field, a flight twelve minutes away. A few years later, she would watch him fall one hundred feet from the sky to his death while testing an experimental biplane.

As the former Mrs. Becker, Edna was one of the first women to fly above Vancouver. Always adventuresome, she sat on the lower wing clinging to a strut. When Silas, four years her junior, flew her from Portland's Oaks Amusement Park to 1,250 feet, the ride sparked her flying bug. Future excursions led to their 1912 marriage, much to their friends' surprise. After a move to San Francisco, she helped her husband prepare planes in his shop.

Before her husband's death, Edna Christofferson promised him she'd solo. Nearly sixteen years later, she did. It wasn't fear holding her back. Her husband trained her and was exacting and critical. Perhaps it was her husband's chastisement during training that delayed her soloing and gaining a license until late 1931. Or maybe it was seeing Silas's tragic crash in 1916 and racing to reach his broken body.

Once widowed, she enrolled in an X-ray class, worked at Portland hospitals and was among the first X-ray technicians in the area. She founded an X-ray school, offering introductory and graduate courses in 1925. Christofferson became vice-president of the national association of X-ray technicians. When a chiropractor falsified an X-ray, she appeared in court, exposing the scam and establishing herself as an expert witness regarding X-rays.

She formed organizations to support women's shooting and flying. A crack shot, Edna advocated for women's self-defense using firearms. As the only female competitor at a 1927 international police competition, she earned second place. In 1928, she started the Oregon Woman's Revolver Club with fifteen members. The women often used the Vancouver Barracks shooting range. The Army awarded Edna an expert medal for making 85 percent of her shots at the barracks. After a competition in New York, where she scored ninety-six of one hundred shots, the New York City police captain called her the best woman revolver shooter he'd ever seen.

In 1930, she created the Women's National Aeronautic Association, where she met famous fliers Dorothy Hester and Edith Foltz. All eyes seemed on

Edna Christofferson delayed getting her own pilot's license until 1931. She founded the Women's National Aeronautic Association to promote women's flying. *Oregon Historical Society.*

the widowed pilot during her solo in 1931. *The Oregonian* reported her plane as a "modern 90-horsepower air-cooled" airplane built for more strain than the rainy day put on it, adding twenty years earlier, planes couldn't fly in a shower. Before ending her solo flight, she flew over the Oregon airfield named for her husband and dropped flowers. Oregon's governor appointed Edna to the state aeronautics board the following year.

In February 1932, Edna flew to Alaska with William Graham to find a lost steamship holding valuable furs. En route, she sent dispatches to *The Oregonian* until she and Graham were lost for ten days on an uncharted Alaskan lake. Newspapers reported daily updates on the search. After searchers found them, both returned to Portland.

Christofferson returned to Alaska the next year to work in two gold mines. She died in Vancouver in 1945. Obituaries listed her as the oldest woman flier at sixty-four, but she was younger, just fifty-nine.

Writer and Humorist: Ann Bohrer (1904–1993)

In a 1991 interview with the *Tualatin Times* in Oregon, Ann Bohrer told the reporter she was born the same year the Wright brothers first flew. She fibbed. She was born more than a month later in January 1904. Still, her birth was close enough to the brothers' first flight that she could fairly claim her life paralleled the growth of aviation, and as a woman she participated in it. Born in Michigan, she claimed herself an Oregonian because her family left Michigan when she was under a year old.

Flying in the *City of Vancouver* Travel Air with Vern Bookwalter, who proudly pocketed a pilot's license signed by Orville Wright, Ann made her first flight. Bookwalter escorted Ann around Pearson Field and then returned, only to crash land. But the ground collision didn't put her off flying.

Uninjured by the flight, Ann decided to become a pilot. The petite brunette and her brother went on to take flying lessons at the Rankin School of Flying in 1927 at Mock's Bottom on Swan Island, a muddy stretch only reachable by boat or airplane or walking precariously over half-floating logs. There she gained the nickname "Half-Pint" due to her small stature. To pay for flying lessons, Ann showed off her stenography skill and became Rankin's secretary and public relations director. Later she used the same tactic to keep flying with Lee U. Eyerly, owner of Eyerly

Ann Bohrer was among the first women in the Pacific Northwest to fly and parachute. She wrote of a nearly disastrous parachuting experience for *Popular Aviation*. *Oregon Historical Society.*

Aircraft in Salem, Oregon, where she eventually became the first official hostess at Salem Municipal Airport.

Ann signed up with the equally petite Faye "Tiny" Carter from Elba, Washington, who, like her, flew with cushions and blocked rudder pedals. Despite their diminutive size, the two were among the first women in the Pacific Northwest to fly and parachute. True to her nickname, Ann couldn't fill the cockpit unless seated on a couple of cushions to boost her high enough to look out of the cockpit. The cushions, however, put the plane's rudder pedals too far from her feet for her to kick a full rudder, making her do a bit of a ground loop as she landed. Seeing this, a mechanic made her a four-inch extension block and added a third pillow behind her back. These "fixes" improved her landings.

According to Ann, the public thought women should be home washing dishes. At the field, the men believed Ann and Faye were out of their element and felt there was no room in aviation for women, she recounted in her oral history. Oliver Judd, who thought women belonged on the ground, was often frustrated by Ann's flying because it was his chore to add the pillows and extensions each time she took a plane up. At the time, pilots reasoned that a woman couldn't fly a biplane because it required too much strength. Ann, however, reasoned that the planes she flew had adjustable stabilizers that could be set to weight, and she'd not fly a plane without stabilization because she wasn't strong enough.

Once, a Swan Island instructor, who had four men ready to solo in one day, was angry when a promising student messed up his flight. He stormed over and told Ann, "They couldn't hit the broad side of a barn" and ordered her to show them how to fly. Ann responded that she'd already been up so she couldn't fly again. He ordered her up. Although she was wearing high heels, she rolled down the cuffs of her white flight suit and ran to the plane, hoping no one would spot her. Seeing the heels, everyone watching knew it was a woman headed for the plane. The instructor told her he'd forgotten to say there was only fifteen minutes of fuel left. So, she took off, flew around the field and then landed, embarrassing the male students into better solo flights.

Ann was the first to solo and land a plane at the still unfinished and unused Swan Island Airport. Rankin insisted that his pilots knew how to parachute and Ann would have to jump, although a few days earlier she'd refused to. In *Popular Aviation*, August 1931, Ann wrote about her first jump, saying, "Looking over the edge of the cockpit at the vast panorama below, the idea of stepping off into space did not, exactly appeal to me." Still, she knew she needed to learn what it was like to bail out.

In 1928, Ann, Faye Carter and Dorothy Hester were the opening for Tex Rankin's air circus. Ann, floating with a red parachute, was the first jumper, making her the first woman in Oregon, if not the Pacific Northwest, to make a jump. Then Carter in a white chute and Dorothy in a blue chute followed. Before the jumps, Rankin and a second pilot tested the air currents to spot where Ann might land while she rode on the leading edge of the plane leaning backward. When Rankin gave her the thumbs up, she pushed off with her feet and fell feet first toward the earth. Ann knew the wind was too strong and she'd not make the landing strip. As she streamed toward the ground, she flipped to her back and finally sped head down.

Looking up past her boots, Ann noticed the twisted chute shroud. Falling, she looked at Rankin, the other pilot and an *Oregonian* photographer in a third airplane. They looked scared. She noticed a "little puff" at the top when suddenly her chute deployed, jerking her feet down, and the shroud lines cut into her shoulders. As the lines unwound, Ann countered with an opposing turn, spinning in a circle and straightening the twisted line.

Ann floated over a herd of cows, shouting, "Shoo, shoo." Then over the Columbia Slough, she feared a water landing, worrying her chute would pull her small body under, drowning her. Next, she floated past the Swan Island Airport, and a grove of trees came into her view. Her chute snagged a treetop, throwing her into a gully, where she hit hard enough to knock her breath out.

Grabbing the shroud lines, she pulled herself up and could hear planes in the air. She was found partially entangled by a boy competing in a Salem to Portland Walkathon. Ann claims her landing left her with bruises for a month. Carter jumped next, only to land in telephone wires, and the fire department had to rescue her. After two bad attempts, Rankin now knew where to let Dorothy Hester out. She floated down in her parachute, landing in the center of the airport.

After Tex Rankin's deadly plane crash in 1947 near Klamath Falls, Oregon, Ann took a civil service exam and spent twenty-nine years working for the Fish and Wildlife Service. Ann was a charter member and co-organizer of Aviatrix International, an organization of pioneer women pilots, based in Birmingham, Alabama. She was also a member of the OX-5 Aviation Pioneer's Oregon Wing and a member of the Portland Aviation Breakfast Club. She was posthumously awarded the OX-5 Aviation Pioneers National Air Woman of the Year. (The OX-5 was a Curtiss-designed, eight-cylinder water-cooled engine that powered early aircraft.)

During a newspaper interview before her 1993 death at eighty-nine, Ann admitted she last flew an Ercoupe, a rudderless monoplane, in 1954. After that, she flew only as a passenger. Ann never applied for a pilot's license and therefore couldn't be accepted by the Ninety-Nines. "Flying is so different today," she told the reporter. "It's no fun flying anymore—it's all rules and regulations."

Not all of Ann's experiences were memorable firsts. She had one extraordinary "last." She was the final woman flier in the United States to have her photo taken with her friend Amelia Earhart, just before the start of Amelia's fatal flight.

DISTANCE FLIER AND FLIGHT INSTRUCTOR: EVELYN BURLESON WALDREN (1908–1986)

Evelyn Waldren always seemed on the move, mostly in lightweight airplanes. She began her aviation career as the first woman to fly in Nebraska and ended it as a grandmotherly flight instructor at Vancouver's Evergreen Airport in the mid-1980s. During the 1930s, she flew in and out of Pearson Field. In the airstream behind her, she left three husbands.

When the *Omaha Bee-News* ran an article in 1928 with a photo of nineteen-year-old Evelyn Nicholas (her maiden name) claiming her as the state's first woman flier, her estranged father of ten years wrote to the newspaper. The *Bee-News* credited its reporting for reuniting them. After they uncomfortably met, Waldren pasted the reunion clipping in her scrapbook, writing beneath it, "He seemed like a stranger." In December 1928, she soloed after fourteen hours of instruction flying a World War I Jenny trainer. Back then, she was already thinking about teaching others to fly and married her instructor, Howard Burleson.

After marrying, the Burlesons operated a small airport in Jamestown, North Dakota. To promote it, Evelyn wrote a local aviation newspaper column about the pilots and goings-on at the airport. Eventually, she managed several airports in California and Oregon, also writing columns promoting them. Her long-running "Wings over the Willamette" for the Albany, Oregon airport appeared in the *Albany Democrat* weekly and promoted the airport, what Waldren was doing and who she was instructing during the late 1930s. She also wrote of her experiences in nationally distributed aviation magazines of the day. She was the second woman in the United States to receive an instructor's rating, which she put to good use at the Albany airport. She was not only a flight teacher at that airport, but she and her husband also served as airport management from 1937 to 1941.

In October 1941, Evelyn Waldren set a nonstop lightweight plane record flying *Lady Liberty* sixteen and a half hours from Vancouver, British Columbia, to Tijuana, Mexico. *Oregon Aviation Historical Society*.

In 1941, she began planning a three-country goodwill flight, starting in Vancouver, British Columbia, and ending in Mexico City. The flight route would be 1,700 miles nonstop in a lightweight plane—something no one had done before. Getting government permits from Canada and Mexico frustrated her, making her announce and cancel the flight several times.

With her permits finally approved, Waldron took off on October 1. Unfortunately, she'd somehow misplaced the paperwork to enter Mexico. After following beacons all night and encountering fog and rough weather, she landed her two-seater across the border from Tijuana the next day. Her sixteen-and-a-half-hour flight was miles short of her goal but still a 1,200-mile nonstop record in a seven-hundred-pound airplane.

Like Edith Foltz, Evelyn Waldren was one of the 117 best women fliers to receive Jackie Cochran's letter to travel to England and ferry aircraft for the ATA during World War II. The women had to find their way immediately to several airports, to the East Coast and then to the United Kingdom. Waldren didn't think she had time to respond. However, Foltz talked her into traveling with her. In Waldren's oral history, she explained her mother and sister threw fits when they heard, so she backed out. However, in a letter to Cochran in 1942, she wrote that her mother possibly had cancer and she felt she didn't want to leave her alone for eighteen months. Instead, she became a charter member of the Civil Air Patrol, training civilian pilots stateside.

Waldren spent her last years teaching students for the Mill Plane Flying Service at Evergreen Airport. Two years before her death, she was recognized as one of eight living women licensed to fly before May 1932. The grandmotherly Waldron was always a promoter of aviation, especially to young women. She gave presentations and encouragement, saying what she had since her first 1928 interview about flying: "It's a good business."

She was a pilot for fifty-eight years and a flight instructor for forty-seven, training hundreds of pilots. When civilian planes west of the Cascades were grounded during World War II, she taught military pilots in Alturas, California. In 1986, the year she died, Waldren was nominated for National Instructor of the Year and was chosen as the Western Region's Instructor of the Year by the Federal Aviation Administration. During her life, she logged 23,700 flight hours.

Record Breaker: Dorothy Hester (1910–1991)

As a child running trying to catch a hot-air balloon floating high above, Dorothy Hester hoped she might hitch a ride with the balloonist. The balloon floated away, leaving the dream of soaring the skies in her mind. She would go on to be one of the best stunt fliers in the nation and hold the record for outside loops for nearly sixty years.

For one day in 1930, July 29, the City of Vancouver leased the Vancouver Municipal Airport. From there, the 1930 Pacific Transport Air Tour would visit twenty-two cities, covering 1,765 miles. The National Aeronautics Association sponsored the tour, and Tex Rankin was flying one of the forty-nine aircraft on the field. The first day of the tour featured an exhibition that included two women, Edith Foltz and Dorothy Hester. Hester flew her signature outside loops. Each loop puts nearly five g-forces on the pilot, and unless restrained by a seatbelt, the pilot would fall out of the biplane on the bottom side of the loop.

Hester's mentor, Tex Rankin, was a skilled and trophy-winning stunt pilot, so it's no surprise that Hester, guided by him, would become a groundbreaking stunt pilot. In 1931, she flew twenty-three consecutive outside loops, setting the women's record. Later in life, she was the first woman to take the U.S. Navy's gravity test for pilots. The testing proved she had an unknown advantage. At a time when six Gs of force was deemed tough on a pilot, she endured 8.6 Gs. The Navy's test revealed Hester's high tolerance for g-forces gave her an advantage in her trademark outside loop stunt, helping her cinch several records.

Her entry into flying was humble. Not able to pay the $250 for flight training or the $25 per flight, the shy seventeen-year-old tried turning to parachuting because Rankin paid $100 per jump. She hoped to earn sufficient money to pay for flight training. But when she attempted a first jump during a Medford, Oregon air show, the pilot had to bash her fingers to make her jump. So, she trained on weekends while working weekdays in a wool mill.

Impressed by her parachuting and flying, Rankin began teaching her stunts; eventually, she conquered an upside-down figure eight. On the PAT tour, she flew every kind of loop—outside loops, barrel rolls and elephant rolls—before large crowds. Then, months later, she broke the men's record with an astounding 125 consecutive outside loops. When asked why she risked her life, she said, "In the sky nobody can tell you what to do. With a good plane there isn't anything you can't do."

Milwaukee, Oregon–born Dorothy Hester received a silver bracelet in 1930 for her stunt flying accomplishments. She held the women's outside loop record for fifty-eight years. *Oregon Historical Society.*

In 1932, Hester joined Rankin's brothers Dudley and Richard as a flight instructor for the Union Avenue Flying Service, an air taxi service and flying school, which closed a month after opening when Dudley died. Next, she opened and ran her own school in Cornelius, Oregon, for two years. She married another Rankin student, Robert Hofer, in 1934. They produced two daughters, and she quit flying. After Hofer died, she married Franklin Stenzel in 1970. In 1989, Hester was in the audience watching Joann Osterud execute 206 consecutive outside loops, breaking her fifty-eight-year-long record. In 2000, she was inducted into the Oregon Aviation Hall of Fame.

8
SKY KINGS

Stunt Pilot and Daredevil: John "Tex" Rankin (1894–1947)

In 1928, a young Portland girl, Carol Mangold, loaned her black cat Alba Barba with one white whisker to a pilot in that year's National Air Race from New York to Los Angeles. The pilot, John "Tex" Rankin, started flying with the number 13 on his Waco 10 biplane fuselage in the national races the year before, attracting more news photos and articles than other participants. He reasoned flying an airplane with the number 13 on the side and adding a black cat would be a "double-barreled jinx." This year, he defied two superstitions while hoping to match his publicity from the previous year's race.

To find one, Rankin chose to delay his departure and hold a "cat day" to procure the blackest one. Rankin convinced three aviation editors from Portland newspapers to ask their readers to present their black cats. Cat day was a yowling, hissing and snarling event. Fortunately, no dog appeared. A part-Siamese cat, Mangold's Alba Barba, meaning "white whisker," was selected to become a famous flying feline.

In 1916, while living in Walla Walla, Washington, Rankin joined the Washington National Guard. Soon, he found himself at the Mexican border in response to Pancho Villa's incursion into Columbus, New Mexico, killing seventeen people. Once General John "Black Jack"

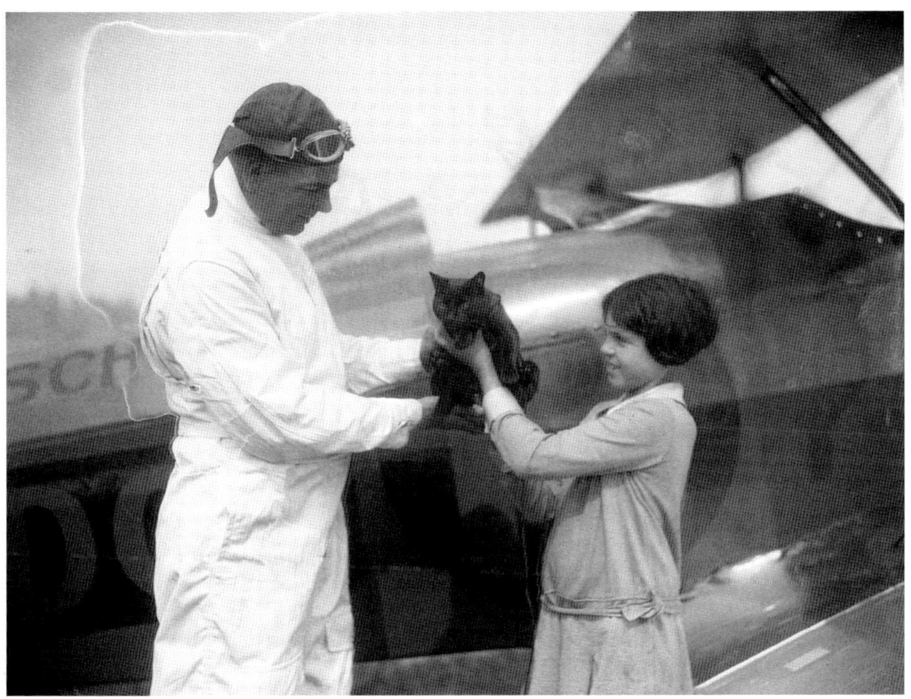

Carol Mangold loaned stunt pilot Tex Rankin her black cat, Alba Barba, for an air race. Rankin flew with the number 13 painted on his fuselage. *Oregon Historical Society.*

Pershing pushed Villa's band into the Sonora Mountains, Rankin returned to fixing Model-Ts in Walla Walla. There, he met a man building two airplanes. Before he could finish the planes and fly them, his National Guard unit went to France.

Before leaving, Rankin passed an Air Corps examination. In France, he attended French air school for three months and next found himself in charge of assembling American-built planes. He and his crew sent over 1,200 airplanes to the front. Although he wasn't a pilot yet, as an aeromechanic, he learned how planes were constructed and the physical forces airplanes underwent during flight.

When the Armistice was declared, Rankin was discharged and returned to Eastern Washington, heading for Spokane, where he signed on with Symonds & Russell Aviation to learn to fly. Rankin did so well that he could fly passengers and accumulate enough cash to purchase an airplane. Next, he established his first flying school. Training seventy Walla Walla pilots, he'd exhausted the market by mid-1922. Still, Rankin gained some modest news coverage and learned the power of publicity. That year, he performed in an air circus with an unknown parachutist named Charles Lindbergh.

Rankin had an eye on Portland for his school because the Oregon and Washington beaches provided lucrative barnstorming opportunities. The Oregon, Washington and Idaho Airplane Company, located in Portland, was struggling and selling off its inventory of thirty-two airplanes. Rankin purchased an Oriole and a Jenny and then worked out a deal to use the field part-time but soon moved his school to Pearson Field. From 1924 to 1926, Rankin ran the school from there while Lieutenant Oakley Kelly was commander. Danny Grecco worked as Rankin's mechanic. As the commercial field at Pearson competed for air contracts, Rankin opened the Rankin Flying Service, offering twenty-four-hour air taxi service at land taxi rates. He also ran scenic excursions to Mount Hood.

Learning that a one-thousand-foot-long and two-hundred-foot-wide runway was available at Mock's Bottom on the east bank of the Willamette River in Portland, Rankin leased it in 1925, leaving Pearson Field. The bottom had been used for exhibition flying in World War I days and was across the river from what would become Swan Island Airport. He soon raised a hangar and painted "Learn to Fly—$250" in large letters on its side. By 1928, Rankin's school was flourishing, and he hired more instructors, including his brothers. When he outgrew Mock's Bottom, he moved to Swan Island briefly while awaiting the nearby development of his new Rankin Field.

In 1928, he decided to test a double-barreled taboo by adding a black cat to the number 13 painted on his plane's fuselage. Alba Barba was a captive on Rankin's plane, which was painted bright red and renamed *The Rose of Portland*. The fuselage number 13 must have been unlucky for the cat. With no place to do what cats do—stretch, scratch and yowl—the engine noise must have gotten to Alba Barba. At the landing in Kansas City, the cat deboarded the plane, freeing himself from confinement. On the hook for Carol's cat, Rankin went cat hunting, finding more alley cats than domestic. Without recovering the girl's cat, he took off for New York. Not long after, the cat followed, forwarded there by his friends.

Black-cat-ology and superstitious 13 didn't work out for Rankin, who finished fifth in the race and pocketed $500 for that status. Upon his return to Portland, Carol met him at the airport and reclaimed her feline, which Rankin was more than happy to turn over. Maybe the cat was lucky—Tex could have finished eighth and gotten no prize money.

Brigadier General Jimmy Doolittle called Tex one of the most gifted aerobatic pilots alive. Rankin won the world aerobatic championship in 1937 and held it for a decade. He set a record of 19 consecutive loops in 1929 and extended it to a record 131 loops. In 1938, he moved to California, schooling pilots at the Rankin School of Flying at the Los Angeles Metropolitan Airport. He trained several entertainers, including Jimmy Stewart, Errol Flynn and Jack Webb. When he decided to teach ventriloquist Edgar Bergen at that school, he refused to teach Bergen's wooden-headed partners, Charlie McCarthy and Mortimer Snerd.

Later, Rankin would claim he foresaw the country going to war and wanted to do something to help. So, he applied to the government for a contract to teach flying. Rankin and his school garnered so much national recognition, the government issued him one to train pilots. The agreement meant he needed more space. He left his Los Angeles school to set up a new one at the Tulare Airpark north of Bakersfield, keeping the Rankin Aeronautical Academy name while changing his focus from training civilian pilots to military fliers. The groundbreaking in February 1941 was followed by forty-five days of rain in the first two months of construction, but 41 men signed up for the first class. Eventually, the school trained 10,450 cadets, 80 percent of whom graduated. Only 5 died.

When running his school in Oregon, he insisted on Pearson Field for soloing student pilots. After the war, Rankin returned to Pearson, selling Republic Seabee amphibious planes out of one of the larger Army hangars there. In 1947, Rankin died after crashing his plane into a powerline while taking off from Klamath Falls, Oregon, in a Seabee amphibious plane. Today, a propellor from one of Rankin's planes hangs in a McMenamin's restaurant in Portland.

AVIATOR AND MECHANIC: DANNY GRECCO (1896–1983)

Dionysus Daniel Grecco led a life in aviation that put him frequently in the right place at the right time. His "luck" likely exposed him to a more varied experience in Pacific Northwest aviation than any other person. His 1912 reassembly of Christofferson's Pusher on the Multnomah Hotel and his 1937 disassembly of the Soviet ANT-25 are but two examples.

Grecco balanced and walked on airplane wings without safety equipment hundreds of feet above the ground. He flew in air circuses and parachuted out of planes. His knowledge about planes inside and out eventually earned him a master mechanic rating, and in 1947, he proved his mechanical expertise when he gained a commercial helicopter mechanic certification—the first issued in the country.

Grecco appeared on the scene for many early and later aviation firsts, starting with the landing of Lincoln Beachey at the Vancouver Barracks in 1905. After rebuilding Silas Christofferson's plane on the roof of the Multnomah Hotel, he watched as the Curtiss Pusher lifted off from a rough-hewn two-hundred-foot plank runway in 1912.

Unfortunately, he was also responsible for the first civilian deaths at Pearson Airfield. In April 1927, he and two passengers failed to lift to the takeoff level needed to clear the railroad embankment paralleling the south side of the airfield. An *Oregonian* headline said Grecco wasn't expected to live and noted "possible internal injuries." He lived. The news report noted the "polyglot" nature of the airplane that Grecco built. However, Tex Rankin told the reporter the plane was in good mechanical shape. The two dead Portland women, Zola Schau and Harriet Franklin, worked for the Pacific

Danny Grecco's life touched aviation high points from Christofferson's flight off the Multnomah Hotel to Vancouver's 1975 memorial of the first U.S. Russian Monument. *Oregon Aviation Historical Society.*

Telephone and Telegraph Company. Apparently, Grecco and Franklin had been dating prior to the accident. At the time, Washington State had no law requiring a license to carry passengers.

The year before Grecco's 1896 birth in San Jose, his parents immigrated to the United States and California. In 1904, the family moved to Portland in time for the impressionable nine-year-old to see Lincoln Beachey's flights to the Vancouver Barracks during the 1905 Lewis and Clark Exhibition. The youthful Beachey flights sent Danny on his course into aviation.

His experiments in flight started at the tender age of ten and showed a budding ingenuity and mechanical interest. He constructed one-to-fifteen-foot-tall balloons made of tissue paper open at the bottom. A pan under his balloons burned kerosine-soaked trash, creating a flame. As the flame burned, heat rose to fill young Danny's balloons, making them rise and float uncontrollably away.

Pedaling his bicycle, he tracked them to where they fell—usually on rooftops or in empty lots—sometimes starting fires. His parents quickly ended these first flight attempts, thus avoiding any legal responsibilities but failing to diminish the youth's aviation gusto. In 1912, the department store Meier & Frank advertised a model airplane contest, which his diminutive Curtiss Pusher won.

Grecco quit school to hawk newspapers, which led to his first tinkering with machines. For his first real job, he serviced race cars and boats for Phil Jackson, son of the *Oregon Journal*'s owner Sam Jackson. Grecco's first plane ride was with Silas Christofferson in the pilot's home-built Curtiss-Parker hydroplane in 1913. Afterward, he saved enough money to buy a fifty-horsepower water-cooled engine to install in his own home-built airplane, flying it at nineteen for the first time in 1915. He was lucky to have landed without injury.

During World War I, Grecco served in the Signal Corps at Mathers Field, California. In the postwar years, his interest in aviation intensified as all the world became aware of the advantages of aviation—and he was ready to spread his wings. In 1919, just twenty-three, he completed a successful solo from the current location of the former Montgomery Ward building in Portland, which led to a half decade of barnstorming around the Pacific Northwest at many state and county fairs for the Oregon, Washington and Idaho Airplane Company, earning between $300 and $1,000 for his performances.

His role there was all-inclusive—he served as a flight instructor, wing walker, stuntman and parachutist. In his later years, Grecco considered his wing walking foolish, despite being choosey about who piloted the plane. He considered the pilot primarily responsible for a successful wing walk.

At the Tillamook fair, the fog rolled in. Instead of canceling, the performers, not wanting to lose their fees, decided to go up two hundred feet so the crowd could still see them. Grecco completed his aerial feats and climbed back into the second plane seat. Attempting to land, the pilot hit a barn, ending up in a pig pen. Both Danny and the pilot walked away muddied, leaving two dead pigs and an angry farmer behind.

In August 1923, Grecco performed a boat-to-airplane stunt between speedboat races. With Grecco riding in the fastest boat, skimming across the water at seventy miles per hour, a biplane dropped a ladder for him and lifted him from the deck. He climbed the ladder and then onto the wing, pulled the ladder up and stowed it in a seat. Then, he walked back on the wing and dived into the river from two hundred feet up.

That fall, Grecco joined a team of four pilots, four mechanics and two interpreters to deliver twenty-eight surplus trainers to China. The trip was funded by Chinese merchants as a gift to their country. The Americans trained young Chinese pilots at the Canton School of Aviation until the next spring. While there, he served as chief mechanic and rebuilt the aircraft. Returning in 1924, he spent nine years as a mechanic for stunt pilot Tex Rankin's school at Mock's Bottom. He met famous friends of Rankin, including Admiral Byrd and Wiley Post, the one-eyed flier.

In *Twenty Smiling Eagles*, Walt and Ann Bohrer recount a Grecco stunt involving parachuting turkeys. This one caught the eye of the director of the humane society. Grecco and a pilot friend, Archie Roth, took turkeys aloft swaddled in small parachutes and dropped the frightened birds from the airplane just before Thanksgiving. Theoretically, the turkeys would float to earth for onlookers to catch along the Columbia River's beach just west of today's Jantzen Beach. Grecco boasted that his turkey bombs would be on target. The flaw in the plan was the "turkey chutes" failed to pin down the birds' wings.

With onlookers lining the riverbanks hoping to catch a turkey for their feasts, the OX-5 Curtiss Jenny and its load of turkeys struggled to get enough height for the first mass parachute jump of all time. Finally reaching the needed elevation, Grecco left his seat and went out to unleash the turkeys tethered to the plane's struts. The result was a "skyfull [*sic*] of flapping, screaming gobblers dragged by windblown parachutes across the entire length and breadth of the county." Some ended up snagged in trees and telegraph wires or fell into sloughs. Others landed at Troutdale a dozen miles up the Columbia. The local humane society was aghast at the turkey droppings and let Grecco and Roth know.

Charles Lindbergh's solo across the Atlantic, landing in Paris in May 1927, brought aviation to the world's attention. In September that year, Lindbergh flew the *Spirit of St. Louis* to Portland, landing at Swan Island Airport, when Grecco serviced the famous airplane. In 1931, when Tex Rankin trained for an endurance flight over Portland, Danny flew the refueling plane. In 1932, the Adcox school hired Grecco for his commercial mechanic license.

He worked on the Bell-X1 rocket plane that Chuck Yeager flew to break the sound barrier in 1947. Selected to be part of the U.S. Geological Survey in 1950, Grecco spent seven years in Alaska ferrying planes for Taylor Aircraft, maintaining Bell helicopters used for surveying.

Grecco bought the plane Basil Russell flew while pioneering the West Coast airmail route, giving it to Portland's Benson High School for educational use in 1958. While he owned many planes, his favorite was his Great Lakes biplane, in which he could perform any stunt. For a decade before his 1983 death, he'd been recognized as the country's oldest fixed-wing airplane mechanic. For his career, Grecco received many aviation honors:

Helicopter mechanic license No. 1 (1947)
Oregon Aeronautics State Board "Top Aviation Mechanic" (1957)
FAA Best Mechanic in the West award (1958)
Oregon OX-5 Club Man of the Year (1959)
Oregon State Board Aeronautics Outstanding Aircraft Mechanic (1968)
Oregon Historical Aviation Society Aviation Hall of Fame (2010)

Danny flew until he was seventy-six, although he'd left barnstorming, stunts and wing walking behind long before. Prior to his 1983 death by cancer, Grecco worked at Pearson Airfield modifying older aircraft. After the Chkalov landing at Pearson Airfield in 1937, he helped disassemble the ANT-25 and pack it up for its return to Russia. He also participated in the erection of the Russian fliers' monument at Pearson in 1975. The year before, Russian cosmonauts Nikolai Rukavishnikov and Anatoly Filipchenko visited Pearson to honor the two Russian landings at the airfield, and Grecco chatted with them, noting that the 1937 flight had only ten or fifteen gallons of fuel remaining when it landed.

THE FLYING FLAPJACK

Pearson Field saw its own unidentified flying object a decade before reports of flying saucers caught the nation's attention at Roswell, New Mexico. Predicting delta wing aircraft, Marvin Joy designed a wingless plane that years later Leverett Richards named the "flying flapjack." It didn't fly far or fast. Joy, an Interstate Bridge tender, designed an arched body, a large fish-like tail for control and rudders behind suspended engines. Joy said the design looked like a pumpkin seed, albeit a very large one. Its front end was ten feet above the ground, resting on two thick tires. Above the wheels were two propellors powered by a forty-five-horsepower Salmson engine. Instead of wings and ailerons, the experimental aircraft used rudders behind its engines to control its flight. Unveiled in September 1937, Joy's prototype looked more like a halibut than a flapjack, pumpkin seed or airplane. At first, the aircraft merely taxied around the runway. But test runs would come soon.

Danny Grecco took the twenty-foot-long, ten-foot-wide prototype aircraft on its first spin around the field. Grecco took Joy's aircraft for a slow test flight around Pearson Field and landed without incident according to an observer of the slow flight, Lowell Moore, an unlicensed flier who was studying to be a mechanic. After Grecco's flight, Joy returned to his workshop to modify his wingless design.

Marvin Joy stands by his wingless aircraft with its twin engines. Danny Grecco made the only successful flight of the aircraft in 1937. *The Historic Trust.*

A second pilot, Sid Monastes, attempted the next wingless flight. Although a professional pilot, Monastes barely got off the ground. He lifted off and then immediately lost altitude, hooking the tail on barbed wire at the east end of the runway. The plane somersaulted. Somehow it landed on its wheels, with the barbed wire wrapped around the tail like a ribbon on a gift package. While Monastes received minor injuries, the flip-over was fatal to the flying flapjack.

Joy's "flapjack" never reached warp speed or broke the sound barrier. It just faded away. Another wingless plane—the M2-F12—didn't fly until 1963. Although Joy wasn't an aeronautic engineer, he consumed "do it yourself" books and articles on everything about aviation. Once he gained a solid understanding of basic aviation physics well enough, he created the wingless aircraft. His experimental plane was backed financially by J.B. Dobson, a colonel in the Air National Guard and manager at Pendleton Woolen Mills.

Winged Journalist: Leverett Richards (1908–2000)

When the military tested a high-altitude B-52's performance at low levels through the heated turbulence of eastern Oregon's high desert in 1959, it crashed. *The Oregonian* sent its aviation reporter since 1935, Leverett Richards, to cover the breaking news and get pictures. The 288-mile trip meant several hours of driving, hiking miles to find the crash site and returning after dark, which doomed the deadline.

Instead of driving, Richards, a pilot, flew, carrying a photographer and an AP technician, making the crash site in an hour and twenty-five minutes. With the photos taken, they hitched a ride to the Burns, Oregon *Times-Herald*, developed the images and sent them over the AP wire in time to meet the deadline. According to Richards, *The Oregonian* was among the first newspapers in the country to cover an entire state.

Born in Colorado and raised in Montana, Richards recalled his boyhood entertainment and education as dependent on books, Chautauqua, traveling shows and rodeos. Those who knew him later would not have guessed that he claimed to be shy and frightened of women. In high school, he and his friends formed homemade skis and skied through Yellowstone Park in 1925, the first to do so.

His first published story appeared in the *Bozeman Chronicle*. It was an interview of General Nelson Miles's daughter, Cecila, whom the youthful Richards called Miss Miles. He knew the general commanded the Department of the Yellowstone but probably didn't realize that he also commanded the Department of the Columbia at Vancouver, Washington, where Richards and his future wife would eventually live.

Richards's education began at Montana State College before graduating cum laude in journalism from the University of Washington. Educated as an old-fashioned journalist seeking "just the facts" and using shorthand to take notes, he eventually moved to Vancouver in 1931, where he joined the *Clark County Sun* as editor. When Richards reported on the city council, George Stoner took issue with his article and challenged him to a duel. As the person challenged, Lev got to select the weapons and deflected the contest by choosing pillows in a phone booth. Two years later, he joined *The Oregonian*, where he worked until his 1986 retirement. Richards's first story appeared

Leverett Richards flew for the Air Force and *The Oregonian* as a pilot, explorer or reporter and visited both poles and seventy-five countries. *Leverett G. Richards Collection.*

in the newspaper in 1931 and his last in 2000. Although he retired in 1986, the newspaper kept him on as a part-time feature writer.

His future wife, Virginia Durkee (1912–2011), was born and raised in Battle Ground, Washington. She graduated from Willamette University with an education degree in 1933. The couple married in 1934 and lived most of their lives in Clark County, eventually building a home on Buena Vista Drive overlooking the Columbia River.

After the Pearl Harbor bombing kicked off World War II, Richards volunteered as an unpaid flight instructor for the Army Air Corps Reserve (later the Air Force) because the Army was desperate to train pilots. His wife took over his job at *The Oregonian* as its Southwest Washington correspondent and photographer until the Army could pay her husband. He served in the U.S. Air Force Reserve, retiring in 1968 as a lieutenant colonel. Because of his smooth head, some called him the "Bald Eagle." Richards participated in three wars: the Second World War as a flight instructor and a B-29 combat pilot; the Korean War in the first operational airdrop in the Arctic; and one Air Force combat mission of the Vietnam War. He was also on patrol with the Navy inspecting remote Army outpost locations in the jungle.

In his book *Elephants Don't Snore*, Richards explained he was a compulsive "storyholic" and enjoyed a "ringside seat on a lot of history in the making." He wasn't bragging. During his fifty-year career, he covered a wide range of news stories, including the construction of the Trans-Alaska Pipeline, the local 1971 hunt for D.B. Cooper, agreements with Indian tribes and landing a seaplane on the Columbia River to cover the 1948 Vanport flood. He circled Mount St. Helens during its 1981 eruption, claiming he wore out three photographers. Lev was one of the first reporters to visit the distant early radar line in the Arctic.

Among his bigger local stories was the 1937 Russian transpolar flight that landed at Pearson Airfield. In 1976, he flew to Pasco, Washington, to cover the fiftieth anniversary airmail flight by Varney Airlines, which initially flew out of Pearson Field and later was merged into United Airlines. Richards traveled to the Arctic and Antarctic poles, visiting the South Pole fourteen times. Whether he sought such adventures or was caught up in them is uncertain. Still, he covered more Pacific Northwest aviation stories in his career than any other writer.

Fifty-five years after the 1937 Russian landing, he covered the story's conclusion at the dedication of the Chkalov Monument, where he met the only living member of the flight, General Georgi Baidukov. The two pilots, both eighty-five-year-olds, swapped stories through a translator. Richards took many of the existing photos of the Russian ANT-25 landing.

The year following that landing, Richards learned to fly at Pearson. Soon after gaining his pilot's license, Richards faced his first forced landing in a biplane owned by a flying club on a return flight near Charter Oak (west of Highway 503 near 279th Street today), about ten miles from Pearson Field. He watched as the plane's sparkplug blew out of the top of the Kenner engine. As his aircraft shook, he envisioned the other four plugs in the five-cylinder engine blowing. Before that might happen, he landed near a barn and called for a mechanic, who repaired the plane and flew it back.

A peculiar 1947 story Richards pursued began when pilot Kenneth Arnold told him he'd seen a UFO traveling 1,200 miles per hour between Mount Adams and Mount Rainier. Soon, a mass hysteria of similar stories was popping up nationwide. As an Air Force Reserve pilot, Richards admitted once being drawn into a UFO chase only to find he pursued a weather balloon. This chase, and other UFO incidents, led him to conclude, "How do you prove something isn't there if it isn't?"

The Oregonian publisher for thirty-four years, Fred Stickel, who died at ninety-three in 2015, called Richards "one of the most extraordinary reporters and writers," whose "expertise as a pilot helped many staffers cover stories in the most remote areas that never would have been reached or reported on. Lev was a strong newsman, right to the very end." Richards flew one thousand hours covering the four corners of Oregon for the newspaper.

When Stickel found that his "one-man air force" was on the payroll for fifty years, he threw Richards a party. Thinking it was a hint to retire, Richards presented his boss with a $10,000 invoice for his flights at a modest $10 an hour at a time when commercial pilots were earning much more. Stickel ignored the bill, knowing that Lev would rather fly than eat. Because Richards was both a compulsive flier and writer, Stickel's paper was likely among the first in the nation to dispatch a pilot across the state to meet publishing deadlines. Eventually, this idea led to helicopter pilots reporting on traffic conditions. Now, we touch a screen to find the same information.

Richards flew for fifty-four years and claims never to have scratched or bitten a passenger, no matter how tempted. Either for the Air Force or *The Oregonian*, Richards served as an explorer, pilot or reporter. When interviewed by William Vallani for the *Oregon Aviation Society Newsletter* in 1997, he had nearly eleven thousand hours of flight time. Besides the North and South

Poles, he visited seventy-five countries. He was part of the crew that made the first airdrop at the South Pole and, in 1956, covered the first landing there. In his spare time, he authored three books: *TAC: The Story of the Tactical Air Command*, *Ice Age Coming?* and his quasi-memoir, *Elephants Don't Snore*.

ILLUSTRATOR AND PILOT: WALT BOHRER (1909–1998)

When Portland lacked an airport, plane-crazy Ann Bohrer found her way to Pearson Field, often with her younger brother, Walt, in tow. At about fifteen, Walt lied to their parents about attending high school at Portland's Benson Polytechnic. His daily attendance was brief. Walt would arrive, walk in one Benson door and out another, then head to Mock's Bottom to hang out with Tex Rankin's pilots. The enticement lay just down the hill from the Bohrers' Portland home. An occasional airplane ride was just too tempting.

Walt Bohrer and Ann appear on a photo addressed to the "Ace of Pilots," a phrase they often used in their communications with fliers. *Oregon Aviation Historical Society.*

Ann wasn't aware of her younger brother's evasive high school attendance, and neither were their parents. When they found out, they didn't fight it but accepted Walt might get an alternative education at the muddy airfield. This decision led to Walt's pilot's license and his acquaintance with his friend and future employer Tex Rankin. Bohrer worked as Rankin's publicist starting in 1925 until the famous pilot died in a 1947 plane crash.

Besides being pilots trained at the Rankin Flying School, Walt Bohrer was also an artist and Ann a writer. In late 1931, he and his sister launched a publication career with a comic book, *Tale Spins!*, that sometimes humorously, sometimes satirically, characterized flying.

Like many pilots, Walt barnstormed. Describing the Curtiss Jenny he flew, Walt said that velocity-wise, you'd do well to hit seventy miles per hour in a speed dive. Mostly, he made enough money to eat and buy fuel to fly to the next town. Walt complained that only the pilot who yelled the loudest sold tickets. Unfortunately, his partner complained of having "frogs and turtles" in his throat, leaving Walt to hawk tickets.

Renowned round-the-world flier Wiley Post barnstormed along the Washington and Oregon coasts with Ann and Walt between his two world-record-breaking round-the-world trips in his Lockheed monoplane, *Winnie Mae*.

Walt and Rankin were fast friends. The artist drew caricatures of the stunt pilot for Christmas cards, showing Tex in a plane with an oversized head and waving. Often the cards featured Rankin's Great Lakes plane with Tex Rankin upside down (so it could be read as Tex did his loopy loops).

Flying in New York as a passenger with Tex, the two spotted a rainbow opening under Niagara Falls at the same time and decided to pass through it in October 1935. On the ground, an official U.S. Department of Commerce car sped up to the two damp fliers, chastising them about their near miss with the cable stretched across the falls. This unsafe flight wasn't the one that took Walt into the National Pioneer Hall of Fame in 1986. But such pilot antics would eventually lead to stricter—and safer—aviation regulations, lacking in the golden age of aviation.

In the late 1930s, Rankin spent time in Hollywood, doing stunt flying for movies and flying with a three-hundred-pound camera and cameraman in the back seat. Hollywood allowed Walt to rub elbows with movie stars Jackie Coogan and Jean Parker and ventriloquist Edgar Bergen.

Walt wrote the only biography of Tex Rankin, *Black Cats and Outside Loops*, much of it based on his 1966 self-published picture book, *Tex Rankin, America's Famous Fliers, a Pictorial History*.

When World War II broke out, Rankin received a U.S. War Department contract to train pilots. He moved his training school to Tulare County, California, renaming it the Rankin Aeronautical Academy, Inc. Walt remained his publicist. Although the school closed at the war's end, Rankin's Academy graduated ten thousand U.S. Army Air Corps cadets. Among its graduates was the star of *Dragnet* (1951–1959), Jack Webb, whose motto was "Just the facts."

FIRST CONTINUOUS INTERSTATE AIRMAIL: VERN BOOKWALTER (1892–1975)

For Airmail Aviation Week 1938, the Vancouver post office created a hand stamp for envelopes sent from the town memorializing the first Post Office–sanctioned interstate airmail and the first airmail in the Pacific Northwest. The cachet honored the 1926 flight from Vancouver to Medford, Oregon, and back. Oregon-born Vernon Bookwalter was the pilot who flew that first Pacific Air Transport airmail run. To his discredit, he piloted the Ku Klux Klan flight over the county's fairgrounds in August 1924.

During the golden age of aviation, "Book," as many called him, was known as a top mechanic, pilot and Alaskan bush pilot. In 1925, he was Tex Rankin's mechanic. Nicknamed "anti-lift" by Tex, the "well padded" Bookwalter also worked for his father-in-law, Jack "Dad" Bacon, in an aviation shack at Pearson Field and for Pacific Air Transport.

Before flying solo, Bookwalter had four hours of Army aviation instruction in 1919. This earned him pilot license No. 82, signed by Orville Wright, which he proudly exhibited. On September 15, 1926, Vern Bookwalter flew the first government-approved airmail round trip for PAT and returned, transporting the first official U.S. Postal mail between Oregon and Washington. Despite his "anti-lift" nickname, Bookwalter cruised from Pearson Field carrying 184 pounds of mail for Medford, Oregon. There he exchanged his plane for another, returning ten mailbags to Pearson Field. Back at the field, a crowd of thousands awaited to see the third time letters had been delivered to Vancouver by air—1905, 1912 and now 1926.

A ceremony two days after Bookwalter's flight launched regular airmail service shredded Vancouver-Portland relations. During the celebration, the jealousy between the more populous Portland and the

Vernon "Vern" Bookwalter flew the first official airmail in the Pacific Northwest from Vancouver to Medford, Oregon, for Vern Gorst's Pacific Air Transport in 1926. *University of Alaska–Fairbanks.*

smaller Vancouver for "ownership" of the route flared. George Baker, Portland's mayor, led a delegation of only Oregonians. Noting this slight, Lewis Shattuck, president of the Vancouver Chamber of Commerce, angrily commented that his city was paying seventy-five dollars a month so Portland received airmail, adding, "and they don't even acknowledge we exist." Gorst cut a deal and agreed to pay a monthly rental until the Swan Island Airport was completed.

On a January 1927 mail flight to Medford, ice forced Bookwalter to land near the Salem State Hospital, which attracted the inmates' attention. The ice broke a wing truss. Someone built a fire and got Bookwalter a hot meal while he waited for a pilot to courier him new parts. He flew with Pacific Air Transport until 1928, when he quit to run his own commercial service.

Modifying planes to carry cargo was dangerous. It not only changed the balance and feel of the aircraft, but tight schedules pushed pilots too far sometimes as well, especially when bad weather, wind, fog and night flights caused delays, increasing the potential for an accident. Two of the northern route's eighteen full- or part-time PAT pilots died in crashes.

Bookwalter flew Walt Bohrer on the youngster's first plane ride. He also took Ann, Walt's sister, on hers in 1927 but crashed when landing. Both walked away uninjured—still, 1927 was a lousy year for Book. That year, he entered the San Francisco to Spokane Air Race. The Vancouver Chamber of Commerce, wanting to promote the city, asked to use his plane for advertising. They painted his plane's blue fuselage with white letters spelling out "The City of Vancouver, Washington." (Even then, there was confusion about the Washington and Canadian Vancouvers.) The chamber believed if Book won the race, it would boost Vancouver's image. Their dream was short-lived.

Betting folks believed Bookwalter had the best chance at winning the race because it covered a route he'd flown many times carrying airmail. On race day, September 21, Book left San Francisco and landed at Medford in first place for a refuel. Then he took off and disappeared. He decided to take a shortcut through the mountains and got lost in heavy fog. He crashed on a mountain. Awaking from unconsciousness, he trekked down the mountain and hours later turned up in Eugene, Oregon. He blamed the wreck on his pigheadedness and a failed ignition sparkplug. His first call went to his fiancée, Esther Bacon; his second was to his mother, who, after the race, he was to pick up in Spokane. Days later, he returned to the mountain to retrieve what he could from the total loss.

Later, he made a mail run forced landing in a field and was worried the cows and horses might damage his plane. Two excited boys who saw the landing ran up to him. Book showed the boys some of the cockpit instruments and then asked them to guard his plane while he got help. When he returned, he found his guards sleeping in the plane. Pacific Air Transport policy forbade giving civilian flights. So, he generously gave each boy five dollars.

In 1934, Bookwalter moved to Alaska. He bought a trimotor Ford from Grand Canyon Airlines of Arizona and then flew it north, where he organized and operated White Pass Airways out of Skagway. He and Esther owned a gold mine near Nome. Vern longed for a warmer weather, but his wife liked the northern climate, so he stayed, carrying passengers and supplies to remote areas of the territory lacking good roads, earning some fame as a bush pilot.

9
BROADER SKIES

Other Airfields

Over the years, Pearson Airfield prompted the emergence of several other airports in Clark County. Evergreen Airfield was the biggest competitor and encouraged middle-class fliers to gather there. Others lasted a while and disappeared, often overtaken by urban growth. Today only two remain capable of continuously handling private aircraft—Pearson Airpark and Grove Field at the Port of Camas, Washington. Still, there are several private airfields throughout Clark County.

Evergreen Airfield

Evergreen Airport allowed loitering. The sign on the door said so, at least until 2006, when it closed, a victim of the changing landscape of Clark County. Once the airfield occupied fifty-nine acres in East Vancouver at 139th Street and Mill Plain Boulevard. Today a ninety-nine-room Hampton Inn sits atop the site. Once the airfield held ninety aircraft, seventy stored in hangars. Evergreen was home base for the Northwest Antique Airplane Club. Eventually, housing encroached on the field and the property had to be sold.

But back in the day, if you visited Evergreen Airport, you'd find aviation enthusiasts to chat with or hear them swapping stories, working on old airplanes and readying them for sale when completed. During the summers, antique airplane races brought national attention to the field. Leah Hing was reunited with her plane at the airport before it closed.

In 1944, the county approved the right to build an airstrip to pilot and attorney Roy Sugg. Mill Plain, at the time, lacked today's boulevard status and was just an oiled road. Sugg sold the property a year later to Waldo "Wally" Olson and Elvin Puckett. They built a one-hundred-foot-wide and two-thousand-foot-long grassy runway. By 1947, they'd added a hangar. As Evergreen Flight Service, they offered pilot training, and soon they had seven instructors, who turned out untold numbers of new pilots. During the 1980s, noted distance flier Evelyn Waldren taught flying there.

As a youth, Waldo "Wally" Olson (1911–1997) built aircraft that never flew and rebuilt them often. Later, he owned Evergreen Airfield. © *Photo courtesy of Gildemeister.*

As Pearson Airpark came into prominence as Vancouver's municipal airfield, Evergreen catered more to middle- and working-class aviators in the east county, providing incentives like discounted fuel prices, building hangars and workshops, then renting these spaces at affordable rates. Evergreen allowed the casual aviator a chance to restore old planes and fly them. About 1970, Olson added a 2,220-foot paved runway parallel to the original grass strip, plus runway lights and hangar tie-down space.

The privately owned but publicly used airport became the casual flier's favorite. In 2001, the airport recorded 200,000 takeoffs and landings. Evergreen Airport fell victim to the Glenn Jackson bridge between Portland and Vancouver, exposing east Clark County to rapid development. Homes, strip malls, apartments and then businesses popped up near the airfield, and noise complaints rolled in. When Olson died in 1997, Mill Plain was a major blacktopped east–west thoroughfare for Clark County. He left the field to his family, who sold it in 2001. Deals fell through until 2007, when one stuck, sealing the airport's fate to development.

Erecting the Hampton Hotel on the former airport site obliterated it—that is, except part of the Evergreen Flying Service hangar. Its front stands at the Western Antique Aeroplane & Automobile Museum in Hood River, Oregon, along with the bench Charles Lindbergh sat on when he visited Evergreen Airport. However, Wally Olson's still airworthy Jenny went elsewhere. It hangs from the Columbia Gorge Interpretive Center's ceiling in Stevenson, Washington.

GROVE FIELD

World War II flier Ward Grove constructed a 2,690-acre airstrip in 1945, two miles north of Camas, Washington, and gave the airfield its name. He started and ran an accredited aviation school there under the Veterans' Program from 1946 to 1959. Grove relocated to Vancouver in 1924 and attended the Rankin Flying School in Portland, acquiring flying skills. Grove was a flight instructor in California during World War II and then returned to Clark County. He sold the airfield to the Port of Camas-Washougal in 1961, and the port commission decided to rename the field in his honor in 1984. Grove died in 1993. On October 6, 2014, a fire at the airport damaged ten hangars, costing $1 million in repairs.

HAZEL DELL AIRPORT

A garage, an airport, a well and a weather station almost changed the name of Hazel Dell, a Vancouver suburb. As a youthful Belgian immigrant, Basil Dhanens (1894–1972) traveled across the country to live with Clark County relatives on their farm. Arriving at Portland's Union Station, he possessed $1.50, black bread, a sausage and a hardened chunk of chocolate. Like many orphans coming west, his name could have easily been forgotten.

On the farm, young Dhanens milked cows and sought jobs. The Thirty-Ninth Street SP&S railroad maintenance shop hired him to pick up parts. Recognizing the boy as bright and hardworking, a mechanic taught him to use a lathe and turned the youth into a machinist.

In 1923, near the intersection of Seventy-Eighth Street and Hazel Dell Avenue, he opened his first business, Basil's Garage, to service Ford automobiles and farm equipment. Later, he moved the garage east to Highway 99.

Bit by the flying bug, Dhanens added a machine shop and built a biplane. During the late 1920s and 1930s, he flew in amateur regional air races. The land near his business became his airstrip and evolved into the short-lived Hazel Dell Airport. Tex Rankin's champion stunt pilot Dorothy Hester commemorated its opening signing envelopes. The envelopes also bore a stamp showing a biplane sandwiched between these lines: "Dedication 'Basil's Airport' at Hazel Dell, on Pacific Highway—Vancouver, Washington, April 15, 1934, Basil Dhanens, Owner, Mgr."

When Basil's Airport closed isn't known. But flying and farming made him acutely aware of the necessity for accurate weather reports. So, he set up his own weather station. From the small six-sided building, he broadcasted daily weather reports each noon for five minutes from a fifty-foot tower. His local reputation as a weatherman grew enough that *Popular Science* featured him in a March 1939 article.

For a while, Dhanens ran a one-man water department. He drilled a 170-foot well on his property and provided nearby homes with water through the 1950s, until Clark Public Utilities took it over. His contributions to Hazel Dell were significant enough that locals wanted to rename it Basilville. He kindheartedly declined.

10

CLARK COUNTY AVIATION STORIES

Did Charles Lindbergh Land Here?

After a solo flight of thirty-three and a half hours across the Atlantic, Charles Lindbergh landed at Le Bourget airfield in Paris on May 22, 1927. Returning to the United States, he toured the nation promoting commercial airmail and passenger travel. His daring flight and the national tour boosted popular interest in aviation for airmail and travel. Pacific Air Transport started airmail flights locally a year before. After Lindbergh's Atlantic flight, its volume increased dramatically.

Charles Lindbergh never landed at Pearson Field but dropped a message in September 1927. He stands by his plane after crossing the Atlantic solo. *Library of Congress.*

Vancouver hoped that he might land his *Spirit of St. Louis* at its historic Pearson Field. Instead, he landed at Portland's Swan Island on the first day of the airport's official opening, September 14, 1927. Once Lindbergh officially opened Portland's Swan Island Airport, piloted aircraft began bypassing Pearson Field. Colonel Charles Lindbergh was only the first.

Construction on Swan Island started in 1926. Once it opened, air traffic bent away from Pearson Airfield to south of the Columbia River. Portland planned a celebration for Lindbergh, including a four-mile parade route starting at the Broadway Bridge and looping around Burnside to Multnomah Field.

Obviously, Vancouver locals felt slighted by the hero's landing on the wrong side of the river rather than their historic Pearson Field. Still, Pearson and southwest Washington weren't totally left out of the aviator's story. There are four stories connecting southwest Washington to the famous pilot: one about a fly under, one about a flyover, one about camping and one about flying Wally Olson's airplane.

As Lucky Lindy barnstormed around the United States promoting commercial aviation, he eventually made it to the Pacific Northwest. Flying down the Columbia River Gorge toward the Bridge of the Gods, Lindbergh supposedly flew under the bridge. For years, rumors lingered about that flight.

But there were four witnesses. One of these, Mrs. Archie Rodgers of Camas, claimed in 1976 that Lindbergh's flight was preannounced, and people gathered at the bridge to see him and take photos. A second, Wayne Mann of Stevenson, was a child and remembered being let out of school to see Lindbergh. Working on a barge on the river that day, Bill Iman said, "We saw Lindbergh go under the bridge." Val Thompkins, lock tender at the Cascade Navigation Canal, wrote that at 1:09 p.m. he observed the Lone Eagle passing down the river "under the Bridge of the Gods. Waved to the operating crew in passing."

Lindy was on his way to land at Portland's Swan Island Airport the first day it was open. At Pearson Field, unlucky thousands of folks stood by expecting him to land there. After all, it was an important army airport at the time. An article in *The Columbian* related that when asked why he didn't land there, Lindbergh retorted he wasn't invited. Still, Clark County wasn't giving up easily. The commander of the local American Legion post, D. Elwood Caples, spoke with Pearson commander Oakley Kelly, a world record endurance holder, and urged him to contact the famous flier in Portland.

Kelly somehow got to Lindbergh and explained the historical significance of Pearson Field. His time filled by the Portland celebration, Lindbergh promised to fly over the field and drop a message on the morning of September 16. To ensure locals knew about the flyover, the Vancouver newspaper reported that a continuous fire siren blast would alert all of

Lindbergh's approach. A crowd gathered at Pearson Field, including children freed from school, anxious to see the *Spirit of Saint Louis* pass over.

On the promised morning, the colonel took off from Swan Island, flying over the Columbia River and above Pearson Field. Circling, he tossed out a weighted message. Caples scooped it up. He had the message framed. For many years, it hung in the American Legion building before it was stored, forgotten and, perhaps, lost.

As reported in *The Columbian*, the message said:

> *Because of the limited time and the extensive itinerary of the tour of the United States now in progress to encourage popular interest in aeronautics, it is impossible for the Spirit of St. Louis to land in your city. This message from the air, however, is sent to express our sincere appreciation of your interest in our tour and in the promotion and expansion of commercial aeronautics.*

Lindbergh did return occasionally to southwest Washington, apparently several times. His brother-in-law Aubrey Neil Morgan, who married Anne Lindbergh's sister Constance, lived in the Ridgefield area. Charles and Anne Lindbergh visited him there. Morgan wrote to the editor of *Clark County History* telling of the Lindberghs' frequent visits. While Morgan couldn't recall the specific dates of these visits, he did remember one in 1948 while he was living in a house on the dike of the Lewis River, saying, "Charles and Anne Lindbergh parked their trailer in a nearby field."

Lindbergh did land at Evergreen Airport sometime in the mid-twentieth century, which was a cherished memory of Wally Olson, its owner. According to a story by Gordon Baxter in *Flying Magazine*, Lindbergh sat in Olson's hangar, saying he didn't want anyone knowing he was in town. Then the famous flier "took a hop in my old Aeronca, paid for it, shook hands and left," Olson told his interviewer. Olson never moved the bench Lindy sat on.

Whether Lindbergh visited the Clark County area again isn't known. The *Spirit of St. Louis*, or rather a replica of it, did land at Evergreen Airport in 1977. Like the original, it flew at 108 miles per hour touring the country, followed by a chase plane carrying all the parts and tools for any repairs. Like other famous Clark County landings, it was unscheduled. The uninsulated, noisy plane was making the rounds to 102 cities for the Lindbergh Commemorative Tour sponsored by the Experimental Aircraft Association.

The flight scheduled was between Ellensburg and Seattle, but bad weather in the Cascade Mountains caused the pilot to fly down the Columbia Gorge. The closeness to the Hillsboro, Oregon airport led the pilot to land at Evergreen. Once the weather changed, the plane continued its circuit. The original *Spirit of St. Louis* hangs in the Smithsonian.

Buried in Lake Vancouver

After World War II, several surplus Mustang F-51 fighters were assigned to the Oregon Air National Guard. One spun into Vancouver Lake in 1951, nearly causing a news blackout. During the lake's dredging, olive-drab airplane parts were recovered thirty years later. Mysteriously, they belonged to an Airacobra P-39. The Mustang remains hidden somewhere in the shallow lake's sludge.

Like its deeper, bigger cousin, the Pacific Ocean, shallow Vancouver Lake doesn't give up dead airplanes easily. The depth of the Pacific embraces them, but the lake's muck entombs them. Two fighter planes crashed into its silty water and disappeared. Neither flew from Pearson Airpark, but one was from the 123rd Fighter Squadron of the Portland Air National Guard and flew out of the Portland Airport. The other's flight remains unknown even after a part of the P-39 curiously resurfaced during the dredging of the lake.

After finishing a gunnery training exercise over the Oregon coast, First Lieutenants Richard Price and Robert Patten flew their F-51 Mustangs back to their Portland base. Each pilot performed slow barrel rolls just before noon over Vancouver Lake. During a roll, Lieutenant Price's aircraft spun into the lake, shattered and sank. He died instantly.

The rescue team hurriedly arrived, followed by reporters and civil and military police. After several hours, the rescuers recovered Price's body, but his plane was rubbish and slid back into the lake. *The Columbian* and *Oregonian* reported the accident in the shallow lake on April 5, 1951.

Military police, aware of the 1947 Roswell media incident and the ongoing Korean War, overreacted, clamping down on the press. They set up roadblocks, called the area a "military reserve" and halted reporters and photographers from viewing the crash site. They threatened to arrest reporters who interviewed witnesses or snapped pictures of the site. They also silenced witnesses.

To dissuade the media, military police demanded Deputy Sheriff Arthur Darby detain an *Oregonian* photographer, Allan deLay, for obstruction. The deputy declined. A second *Oregonian* photographer, Carl Vermilya, landed near the shore in a seaplane. After rapidly snapping photos, he turned and pitched his camera to the pilot, who shuttled it back to Portland.

The next day, a *Columbian* headline bellowed, "Gestapo in Our Midst?" The attempted media suppression caught national attention. The American Society of Newspaper Editors warned four hundred editors a few weeks later, demanding they fight any "arrogant suppression of news" by the government.

Locals forgot the F-51 disaster for three decades. Then in 1982, contractors received a $17 million agreement to dredge a twelve-foot-deep trench around the lake and dump the tailings in the lake's center, forming a small island. The workers understood they might uncover the airplane.

On December 29, 1982, near the mouth of Burnt Bridge Creek, the dredger's clamshell shovel lifted out a battered chunk of aluminum with hinges on one side. Its olive-drab paint suggested a 1940s fighter. Was the wrecked F-51 found?

The piece was sent to federal aviation officials for inspection, who declared it was the cockpit door of a World War II Airacobra P-39 single-engine plane. No one is sure how the P-39 got into the lake. Between 1939 and 1950, local papers reported regularly on other crashes of that model, but none mention an accident anywhere over Clark County. However, the Aviation Safety Network has record of a midair collision of a Bell P-39N Airacobra three miles north of Vancouver that killed the pilot. It occurred on August 13, 1943—Friday the Thirteenth.

So where is the Mustang? The dredging missed it, perhaps even buried it under the lake's new island. Or it may rest shrouded in mud, hiding for a future archaeologist to discover.

Columbus Day Storm, 1962

Angry Freda, a typhoon, battered Washington and Oregon on October 12, 1962. About two weeks earlier, it formed just north of Wake Island. Pacific weather stations watched its increasing fury. With a spin that began just far enough north of the equator, it combined twists with the spinning of the

The 1962 Columbus Day Storm was a typhoon. It ripped over Pearson Airpark, flipping planes across the former polo field, while also damaging Vancouver. *Clark County Historical Museum.*

earth, creating what's called the Coriolis effect, which is associated with large-scale weather events.

Even those who lived through Freda's wrath diminish it, calling it the Columbus Day Storm or the Big Blow. But Freda was a typhoon, a corruption of a Chinese word meaning "violent winds."

When Freda arrived, its ferocity devastated cities and towns more than one hundred miles inland along the Pacific coast from Canada to California. The typhoon doused the San Francisco area in rain falling so fast it created floods and mudslides. It disrupted power, leaving some without electricity for weeks. Portland's KGW-TV lost its power and couldn't broadcast for days.

When Freda assaulted Clark County, Pearson Airpark, the City of Vancouver's official wind site, recorded gusts exceeding ninety miles per hour. C.J. Moss, a veteran weather observer, clocked faster winds—ninety-two miles per hour. Portland officially measured eighty miles per hour. Regardless of the wind's exact speed, Freda crumpled three-quarters of Pearson's planes. They looked like crushed aluminum cans pushed into piles and flipped topsy-turvy, as if they'd crashed on the airfield. The typhoon left one standing ridiculously on its nose.

VANCOUVER'S AROUND-THE-WORLD FLIGHT

In June 1977, an around-the-world flight took off and returned in November. Paul Christensen of Vancouver, a property company owner, and Warren "Rusty" Rogers, his former flying instructor and a Vietnam helicopter pilot, were on board the single-engine aircraft.

Taking to the air after a memorial service, they were honoring the fortieth anniversary of the 1937 Russian landing at Pearson Field. The celebration was arranged by the Vancouver Transpolar Committee, which had invited seventeen Soviet journalists, writers, scholars, engineers and government officials, including the Soviet San Francisco Consulate.

The pair circumnavigated the globe in 161 days, less than half the time of the Army's first around-the-world flight in 1924. Although their trip didn't have the drama of being the first, that didn't mean it was easy. Christensen and Rogers had several adventures. They stopped in Japan and Taiwan and hoped to fly into Russia, but they met with official difficulties with the Soviets, who wouldn't return Christensen's certified mail—somewhat ironic given many were at the airfield on the celebration day before they took off and the journey commemorated the fortieth anniversary of Chkalov's over the North Pole flight.

Paul Christensen (*left*) and Rusty Rogers began an around-the-world flight after the 1975 Russian monument fete. Upon returning, they landed near Pearson in the Columbia River. *From* The Columbian.

The fliers encountered armed guards and water buffalo in India. Once they nearly ditched their plane. They violated airspace over Bulgaria, and a Soviet MIG forced them to land. Twelve Bulgarian officials interrogated them. To resolve the airspace dispute, the forty-three-year-old Christensen was forced to sign a document apologizing for the error. They also flew past Mount Everest at twenty-three thousand feet, eventually stopping in Scotland on the last portion of their $20,000 flight to Vancouver.

When they finally returned home, they onboarded wearing blue skin-diving suits and face masks, tossed an inflatable raft out and were greeted by nearly seventy-five people and a Clark College band of six. The seaplane's fuselage bore paintings of nearly a dozen flags of the countries they touched. Regrettably, the Soviet Union's flag wasn't among them.

CIVIL AIR PATROL IN CLARK COUNTY

Harry K. Coffey was a founder and pioneer of the Civil Air Patrol who lived in Clark County. He volunteered to help monitor the Mexican border during World War II. In 1911, at the age of fifteen, he built and flew a glider before creating and piloting his own plane two years later. He earned his pilot's license in 1914 and served in the Air Corps during World War I. Following that, he linked his insurance business to flying, keeping the Mutual Benefit Insurance Agency's disparate locations connected. He perished in 1954 when his single-engine Beechcraft crashed due to strong turbulence into the Columbia Gorge near Hood River, Oregon. After the 1937 Russian ANT-25 landed at Pearson Field, he collected the papers demonstrating that the Russians flew nonstop from Moscow to Vancouver.

Created in December 1941 by presidential authority under the Office of Civil Defense, the Vancouver Squadron came to life in September 1942 in the back of Art Whitaker's building at Pearson Airport.

Accidents (Some, Not All)

The first fatal accident was a military one. In June 1926, Oakley Kelly gave Lieutenant Henry Goode permission to fly his De Havilland DH-4. Goode took along Lieutenant Julius Syfford, a reserve officer with post quartermaster duties. After they rose two hundred feet over the ground, flames shot out of the plane's right exhaust. Goode banked the plane to turn around, and it slipped out of the bank and hit the ground and exploded in flames. The plane crushed Goode. Syfford was pitched from the plane, dying of burns. Investigators blamed a connecting rod for the crash.

In April 1927, Danny Grecco was flying two Portland telephone operators in his ninety-horsepower biplane. Neither wanted to fly alone. At about two hundred feet after takeoff, the plane plunged into the railroad embankment on the south side of the field. Both women died on impact. The seriously injured Grecco recovered at St. Joesph's Hospital. Police failed to prevent souvenir hunters from carrying off parts of the wrecked plane.

That same year, Vern Bookwalter crashed his Travel Air after taking Ann Bohrer on her first airplane flight. Both walked away uninjured.

Two years later, Lieutenant Ralph A. Floyd crashed in a landing approach, dying instantly. His passenger, Asa Clements, a Portland police lieutenant, died a few hours later. Floyd, a 321st Squadron member, appeared to make a turn too slowly, crashing the plane. The field commander, Carlton Bond, had the crash investigated. Seeing the results, he called it just one of those things that happen.

In July 1929, a new barracks recruit landed in the Columbia River with his parachute and drowned. Conrad Blatter had previously spoken with other enlistees about a parachute. He made the jump from a civilian plane, making what appeared to be a perfect descent. The wind blew him over the river, and entangled in the silk, he drowned. Despite some conflict over the death, the pilot, Charlie Mears, was exonerated.

On August 4 that same year, an inexperienced glider pilot had a serious crash. J.W. Ruben of the Portland Glider Club was towed by a car at the field. The cable didn't release, and he panicked. The craft took a steep dive from about thirty feet above the ground, and Ruben fractured his skull.

On January 29, 1930, the day Varney Airmail pilot Walter Case's body was found, another flying misfortune occurred at Pearson Field. A Rankin Flying service instructor, Fred Sauer, who flew regularly at the field, and a student pilot crashed. They were practicing spins over the Columbia River and failed to pull out of a dive. Sauer's death was likely due to the weight of his flying suit and parachute, but the student survived.

Tektronix lost a co-founder in a 1971 crash. Melvin "Jack" Murdock (1917–1971) was a Portland businessman, philanthropist and radio technician who cofounded Tektronix Inc. with Howard Vollum. The oscilloscope manufacturer they started is now part of the Everett, Washington–based company Fortive. Murdock learned to fly in 1954 through a Tektronix-hosted flying club. Outside of work, he was an avid aviator who flew out of Pearson Airfield.

He enjoyed flying both professionally and recreationally. He used his own plane sometimes for work flights but flew mostly for the fun of it, often in his favorite plane, a Piper Super Cub. In the mid-1960s, his Pacific Northwest Aviation was the largest firm at Pearson Airpark. He also created Melridge Aviation there, Piper Aircraft's distributorship in eleven western states and Alaska.

On May 16, 1971, Murdock died in a floatplane accident on the Columbia River. According to reports, heavy winds caused the Super Cub to flip while taxiing on the water near Maryhill, Washington. Murdock put extra auxiliary fuel tanks in the wings, making the plane top heavy. Because the fifty-three-year-old's corpse was never located, he wasn't pronounced legally dead until June 1971. The Jack Murdock Trust donated a large sum to the Pearson Museum, adding to its name "The Jack Murdock Aviation Center."

II

MUNICIPAL AIRPORT EMERGES

Since its beginning, Pearson Field has endured a shared existence: first between polo games and an aviation camp, next between flying and spruce production. For decades, it was split between military and commercial aviation, its ownership muddled by leases. It wasn't until the Army departed and Vancouver Municipal Airport was dominant, the ownership finalized and shared with the city and the National Park Service, that it became a stable airport. Yet even today its existence remains tenuous.

Municipal Airport Evolves

Several aspects make the history of the airfield confusing when trying to establish who owned what and when. It began as an unnamed "aviation camp" on the Vancouver Barracks polo field. The idea of a runway and the designation *airport* were nonexistent in the beginning. Airports, rather landing strips, were level, wide expanses of grass. Unlike now, when everything happens one at a time, back then multiple planes could land or take off simultaneously. In the beginning, Pearson Field was used as an Army installation and polo field. The placement of the polo grounds was ideal for a landing zone.

Then the polo field was taken over in the First World War by the Army's Spruce Plant, providing the raw lumber for airplane manufacturing. In 1922, when the 321st Squadron arrived, it had a generic name, the barracks field, the flying field and the Vancouver Barracks Aerodrome—the Spruce Plant was gone. The Aerodrome wasn't dedicated until 1925 as Pearson Field, an Army Air Corps flying field. Despite the Army's presence, others started using the field for commercial purposes, like airmail and cargo as well as passenger delivery. At this point, various terms were applied to it—city field, municipal field and, confusingly, Pearson Field—until it was dedicated in 1930 as the Vancouver Municipal Airport.

The Vancouver Commercial Club realized that a commercial field would be a boon to the local economy and wanted to establish a commercial field before its rival on the south side of the Columbia River could build one. In the end, Portland scooped up more airmail contracts and built a larger airport on Swan Island and Pearson shrank.

It was once known as Pearson Airpark before becoming Pearson Airport. In fact, even now that it's an airport, locals still call it Pearson Field. Later, when aviation became more organized and airports were identified as specific sites, runways and associated magnetic headings appeared. Even though it was common practice to land on grass, runways were soon paved, and gravel started to be used. For example, Pearson Field was not paved until 1966.

With the entry to World War II, the 321st Observation Squadron was pulled into active duty, and Pearson Field became a parking lot for jeeps and trucks. However, an emergency gravel landing strip remained. After Benito Mussolini's death and Italy's surrender in 1943, Italy was technically no longer an enemy. The Army shipped nearly fifty-one thousand Italian POWs to twenty-seven internment camps in twenty-three states. One site was the Vancouver Barracks. In 1944, the War Department renamed these camps Italian Service Units. The POWs, technically cobelligerents, stayed in old barracks buildings at Camp Hathaway and in two hangars at Pearson Field. African American soldiers headed overseas were housed separately at Camp Hathaway (located about where Clark College is today). The Italians' day started early and followed routine and discipline like barracks soldiers. Despite imprisonment, the Italians' attitudes remained upbeat, for their war had ended.

The POWs worked on Vancouver Barracks and Pearson Field grounds and off post as military need dictated. Some labored as gardeners, carpenters, warehousemen, launderers, dock workers, even cooks. They received payment for any work. Officer POWs collected $40 and enlisted men $24 a month. One-third of their income came as cash, and the

Dressed in khaki and bearing "Italy" sleeve patchers, the Italian cobelligerents appear to be in a woodworking shop at the Vancouver Barracks. *Clark County Historical Museum.*

rest was issued as scrip (a substitute for legal tender) redeemable at the post exchange or theater. A financially aware prisoner could deposit his coupons in a trust account.

In 1949, the City of Vancouver took over the airfield. The year before, the army declared it surplus and combined the military and civilian properties into one. It evolved into a general aviation airport, and it acquired a paved and lighted runway 3,275 feet long plus instrument guidance with assistance from Portland Airport across the Columbia River.

In 1995, the Vancouver City Council changed the Pearson Airpark to Pearson Field. It exists today in an almost original state like no other Army Air Corps field. Most Army airfields from the interwar period either perished or were so drastically altered that their previous feeling is imperceptible. One example is March Field, which began like Pearson and then rapidly grew into a big aviation complex. Other airfields, including Bolling, Wright and Kelly, have undergone comparable changes. Once an airfield like Pearson, Bolling Field in Washington, D.C., is now overgrown with support facilities, its original runways gone. It's possible that Pearson Airfield is the sole pre–World War II Army airfield. It still maintains many of its original structures, including a historic hangar and headquarters building. Much of the airfield's original design could be restored.

Pearson Airfield's pioneering role in aviation is widely documented. It has a vital link to international aviation and the start of commercial airline services. The 1924 around-the-world flight landing at Pearson brought worldwide attention. The 1929 and 1937 Russian landings at Pearson Field became global events. Valery Chkalov remains a Russian national hero important in the history of aviation. The 1975 dedication of the Chkalov memorial remains an important local attempt to strengthen ties with the Soviet Union's aviation community. Pearson values its links to Russia and the global aviation community. Few aviation facilities or museums in the United States have such an important relationship.

12

PEARSON AIRFIELD STAYIN' ALIVE

The first dedication of Pearson Field in 1925 made 2025 the one hundredth anniversary of its continuous use as a dedicated airfield. In truth, it stretches back to the 1905 landing by Lincoln Beachey at the Vancouver Barracks, just two years after the Wright brothers' first flight, linking it to the earliest days of American aviation. Admittedly, between 1905 and 1912, Pearson Field lay fallow waiting for its first daring aviators to cobble together shellack and spruce aircraft that were never more than prototypes and so unreliable they sometimes didn't make it aloft. In 1911, it was officially recognized as an "aviation camp" by the local paper. These pilots working there were certainly amateurs, likely barely more than enthusiastic hobbyists, willing to risk their lives to circle above the grassy polo field and gaze out over the Columbia River, Mount Hood and the vast stretches of timber that still covered much of Clark County. The risks they took excited the local men and women about the promise and dangers of aviation. Some of them found themselves sitting on a wing or in a cockpit.

Even before reaching its first century, the airpark celebrated many things. The field was dedicated twice, in 1925 as Pearson Field for military use and the second time as Vancouver Municipal Field for commercial use. Pearson Air Museum sponsored re-creations of the 1912 flight off the Multnomah Hotel and the first interstate airmail delivery. The airfield gained world attention when the Army's first around-the-world flight landed there multiple times and then twice again as the Soviets landed in 1929 and 1937, opening the opportunity for the first Russian monument in the United States and the slow melting of Cold War tensions between the two nations.

Over the years, volunteers added their skills and imagination to create a scale-model diorama of the Spruce Mill, models of old aircraft and replicated aircraft for exhibit, including a Curtiss Pusher and a Jenny JN-4. Leah Hing's plane found its circuitous route back to the Pearson Museum, where it was once hangared, and stands in the exhibit hall. The stories of these and the men and women who dared to fly live on through Pearson Air Museum.

AIAA Award

In 2012, the American Institute of Aeronautics and Astronautics recognized the field as a historic aerospace site. Pearson Airpark celebrates two anniversaries since its official dedication in 1925 by the Army and its 1930

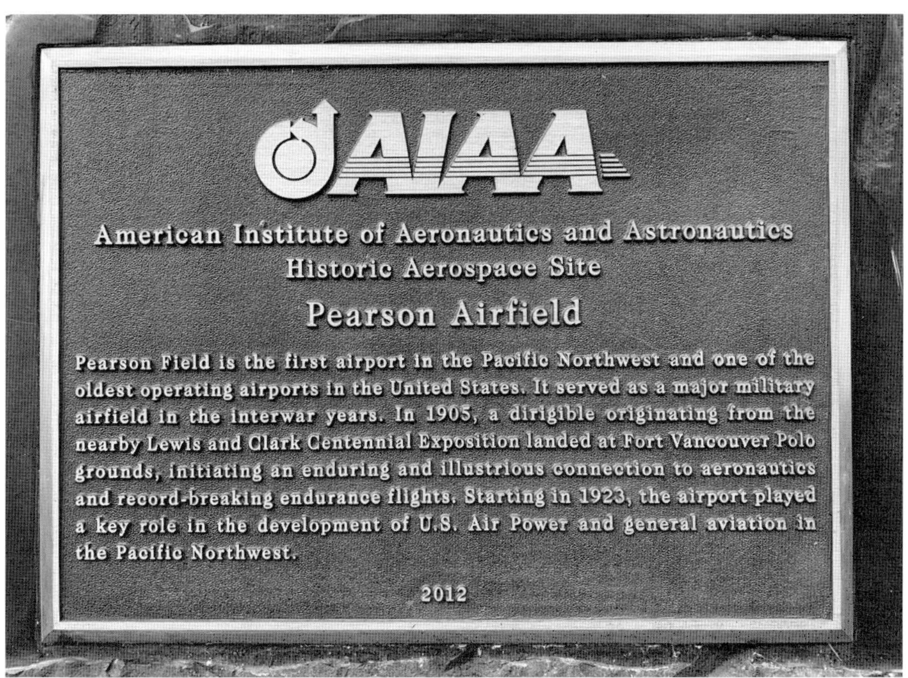

The AIAA declared Pearson Field a historic site in 2012. One of the earliest U.S. airports, it was a key military airfield during the interwar period. *Author's photo.*

dedication as a municipal airfield. Its first one hundredth anniversary coincides with the two hundredth anniversary of the Hudson's Bay dedication of Fort Vancouver on the Columbia River. These events celebrate an area used for transportation and trade for hundreds, if not thousands of years.

EIGHTY-YEAR-OLD FLIGHTS REENACTED

Before his death, Thomas "Tom" Murphy (1946–2023) was once the only Curtiss Pusher pilot in the Pacific Northwest, possibly the country. The antique airplane pilot and mechanic flew down the Columbia River Gorge from the Western Antique Airplane and Automobile Museum in Hood River (WAAAM), Oregon, to celebrate the anniversary of two flights with reenactments. Collector Terry Brandt founded WAAAM as a nonprofit organization in 2006, opening the museum a year later. Today, it contains one of the largest collections of airworthy antique airplanes. The ninety-five-thousand-square-foot building holds nearly 200 airplanes, many still able to fly. It additionally has 210 antique autos and 30 motorcycles. Most are drivable.

Murphy's trip down the Columbia Gorge to Portland may have been rough, but not as rough as replicating the 1912 flight off Portland's Multnomah Hotel (now Embassy Suites) on Southwest Pine. The Federal Aviation Administration didn't exist until 1958 and thus had no say in the first hotel flight. In 1912, Silas Christofferson needed only the agreement of the hotel management. In 1995, the hotel management was willing, but Murphy and his Pearson Field team faced much red tape involving Portland, its police department and the FAA.

An odd question asked by the FAA involved an antique photo of the flight that captured men with a movie camera with a sign reading "Oregon Motion Picture Co." Perhaps the regulators hoped the film might answer some of their questions. Unfortunately, the movie made eighty-three years earlier wasn't found and was presumed lost. Considering the frame rate of sixteen to twenty-four per second at that time, it might not have disclosed some of the hoped-for information if the frame rate was at the lower end. Today, twenty-four frames per second is standard.

The second flight off the Multnomah Hotel was part of fundraising for the Pearson Air Museum. Murphy's flight, however, did more to increase awareness of the museum than fund it. While Pearson Field awaited

Murphy's landing, there existed what Pearson Air Museum manager John Donnelly called a "mini-carnival." The awaiting crowd enjoyed the early 1900s ambiance—a pancake breakfast, five-cent hot dogs, horseshoes and a barbershop quartet—as they waited. Murphy's 1995 flight used a 1947 replica of the Curtiss Pusher biplane flown by Christofferson, one of the few around.

At first, the FAA was dubious about the flight off the hotel, but it eventually provided all the necessary permits—so did the City of Portland and police. Terry Kapan for Hillsboro Helicopters pulled the cables attached to the Curtiss Pusher, lifting it to the top of the hotel and settling it on the wooden plank runway, where it rested until the flight. Low clouds and misty weather nearly canceled the event.

Murphy readied himself at Pearson Field by practicing the short two-hundred-foot liftoffs the rooftop allowed. In the video *Flight of Fancy*, you see the forty-nine-year-old lift off the hotel toward Pearson Field. The liftoff shows the pusher dipping after the plane leaves the timber runway, the tail missing the roof's edge by only a few feet. That scary moment passes once the plane rises, cruising over Portland. Helicopters flanked the right and left side of the pusher. Like Christofferson, Murphy landed at Pearson Air Park twelve minutes later before an excited crowd. Christofferson landed quietly on the polo field. Murphy may have wished for that, but soon after landing,

After launching off a hotel roof, Tom Murphy cruises over Portland headed for the Vancouver Barracks in a fundraising event for the Pearson Air Museum. *From* The Columbian.

jet flights from Portland International Airport blasted above, silencing the pusher's engine noise. The following year on July 4, Murphy flew a P-51 as part of a Pearson Field holiday attraction.

The flight off the hotel wasn't the antique airplane pilot's first Pusher flight. He completed his first three years earlier, emulating the August 1912 flight of Walter Edwards carting the first interstate airmail in the Pacific Northwest and possibly the nation. Eighty years to the day, Tom Murphy completed the same flights Edwards did in a Curtiss Pusher. The idea came from the then-manager of the Pearson Air Museum, Gary Thompson. The aircraft was owned by Terry Brant of Hood River, Oregon, and called "rickety but reliable."

Specially designed envelopes noting the event were canceled in Vancouver. They were sold for three to five dollars each to raise money for the air museum. The museum bought five hundred Glenn Curtiss thirty-five-cent stamps from a New York stamp collector for the envelopes imprinted with a commemorative design. The U.S. Postal Service placed a trailer near the landing sight to hand-cancel the letters.

The lightweight 670-pound aircraft contained a small eleven-and-a-half-gallon fuel tank, giving it a range of about one hundred miles. In 1912, fuel distance was less of a problem than the weather, and Edwards had encountered many bumps along the way. For this flight, a Continental engine replaced the original OX-5 on the pusher, generating a top speed of fifty-five miles per hour.

On August 10, Edwards flew 1,500 pieces of mail from Portland's Waverly Country Club to what would become Pearson Field. He flew 2,000 pieces of mail back to the club the following day. Instead of leaving from a country club, Murphy lifted off from Portland International Airport in the thirty-foot wingspan Curtiss Pusher headed across the Columbia River to Pearson Airpark. Among the payload of letters was one letter from Portland's Mayor Bud Clark.

And what was the flight like? Murphy explained, "Imagine sitting on a lawn chair on top of a telephone pole going down a freeway at fifty miles per hour." Add to that he wasn't wearing a parachute. He admitted the trip was a bit scary when the plane suddenly dropped ten to fifteen feet when he hit an air pocket several times.

BUILDING A CURTISS PUSHER REPLICA

The first mass-produced airplane, the Curtiss Pusher, was a significant influence in early aviation between 1911 and 1914. Designed by Glenn H. Curtiss, Pushers were common during summers at the Vancouver Barracks aviation camp. Glenn Curtiss designed a rear-facing engine, placing it behind the pilot, which gave the "Pusher" its name. The reason for a rear-facing propeller "pushing" the airplane involves a weakness in early engine technology. Oil leaked out of the engines. In front of the pilot, oil spray could obscure his vision. By positioning the engine behind the pilot, Curtiss kept the pilot's goggles and face free from oily mist.

An engine specialist and motorcycle racer, Curtiss broke the speed record for a motorcycle rider, hitting 136 miles per hour, and turned his engine-building expertise into flying in 1907. As a pioneer of aviation, Curtiss created remarkable aircraft and received one of the earliest pilot certificates from the Aero Club of America in 1911. Since permits were distributed alphabetically, Orville Wright received No. 4, and his brother Wilbur No. 5. The FAA first granted federal pilot licenses in 1927, which started the present licensing system.

Volunteers spent seven thousand hours over two years constructing a Curtiss Pusher replica of the Silas Christofferson 1912 biplane now displayed at Pearson Air Museum. *From* The Columbian.

Pilots like Silas Christofferson, Charles Walsh and Walter Edwards piloted these aircraft. Today, the Pearson Air Museum at Fort Vancouver National Historic Site houses a full-scale replica of Christofferson's 1912 Curtiss Pusher, echoing his flight from the Multnomah Hotel to Vancouver Barracks.

The full-scale model of the Curtiss Pusher, currently on display at the Pearson Air Museum, was built in a warehouse by a talented team of National Park Service volunteers, using original Curtiss Aeroplane and Motor Company plans. They also consulted historical articles on early airplane construction, a copy of the 1912 *Build and Fly a Curtiss Aeroplane* instruction booklet and photos of Christofferson's airplane. The volunteers worked two days a week for two years between 2016 and 2018. In total, they spent seven thousand hours researching and constructing a full-size replica of Christofferson's 1912 aircraft.

To produce the most accurate copy conceivable, the builders rediscovered century-old construction methods employed by the earliest pioneering aviators. The volunteers used period-appropriate building methods and materials—such as Sitka spruce, bamboo, steel tubes and cotton fabric—supplied by the National Park Service. Because many of the craft's parts weren't available, they were 3-D printed. Pearson Air Museum has no intention to fly its Pusher, which is on permanent display, although it is equipped with an original engine, a Curtiss OX-5 V-8 block. Instead, the aircraft will remain on static display.

There were no remaining original Curtiss Pushers the volunteers could examine and reverse engineer. To get started, the team members used blueprints from a previous project—a miniature model of the Pusher that a few original team members had built earlier for the museum. For their first effort, they scaled down an original Pusher design, looked through old photos of Christofferson's flight, discovered some slight variations in tail surfaces and found its wings had not twelve sections but fourteen. The added ten feet of wing gave the pilot extra lift off the hotel. The total length of the wings is approximately forty-four feet.

Although there are many individually made components, the team's seven primary members offered a diverse range of abilities and passions that were up to the task. Everyone approached it a little differently. Volunteers from various professions brought their different experiences and talents to the project. One was a physician, two were manufacturing engineers and one was a carpenter. A toolmaker duplicated the replica Curtiss OX-5 engine parts. One of the manufacturing engineers fabricated the hundreds of unique metal parts needed. Another volunteer focused on research and high-quality historic photos.

Unlike Christofferson's Pusher, this aircraft will never fly, since the engine is a reproduction and mostly made of wood and plastic, although the wings would provide enough lift. Two 1912 aviation-grade Champion spark plugs are among the two engine parts that are authentic to the period. Sigma Designs donated time on a 3-D printer and the materials required for replicating the Pusher's carburetor.

During their work, the volunteers discovered modernity wasn't always friendly toward building antique aircraft. In the early days of aviation, builders made their own shellac from shellac beetle excretions, mixed with alcohol. The DIY shellac stiffened the aircraft cotton fabric, shrinking the cotton, waterproofing and preserving the skin. Since then, scientists have bred cotton for shrink resistance. Today, nobody wants cotton that shrinks, except for those building models like this one. The modern cotton wrinkled, requiring the volunteers to resort to a commercial heat gun to smooth the fabric.

PEARSON AIR MUSEUM AND PEARSON FIELD

Today, Pearson Air Museum resides within the Fort Vancouver National Historic Site and is managed by the National Park Service. Pearson Airpark's 134 acres is divided between two owners today. The City of Vancouver owns 62 acres and the National Park Service 73. The city is responsible for the airpark's municipal field and has 150 T-hangars for rent. The field has a full-time manager and offers fuel, flight lessons and tie-down facilities.

According to the Washington State Department of Transportation Aviation Division, Pearson Field and museum attract nearly 40,000 visitors to Vancouver each year, generating $27 million in revenue and supporting around 460 employees. Pearson Field gets no operating financing from the City of Vancouver and is funded entirely by airport users.

The Pearson Air Museum introduces visitors to the history of early aviation, illustrating how Pearson Field contributed to the early days of flight and providing them deeper insights into the golden age of aviation, from its beginnings to its emergence as a military airfield, to its history as the home of the Spruce Mill and its metamorphosis into a civilian field. It is one of the oldest—if not *the* oldest—airports in continuous use in the country.

Beautiful hand-painted murals and exhibit panels, including a diorama of the Spruce Mill, antique planes and a Russian aviation gallery, all fill in gaps found in general aviation histories. Five early twentieth-century airplanes depict the extraordinarily fragile, intricate and adventurous character of early aviation, adding realism to events that occurred nearby. They include the volunteer-built Curtiss Pusher, a JN-4 Jenny, a DH-4 Liberty plane and a 1931 Fleet Model 7 owned by Leah Hing, the third Chinese woman to get a pilot's license.

Outside the grounds, visitors find a statue of Carlton Bond, a monument to the 1937 transpolar Russian flight and several historic buildings, including a hangar and administration building. A third monument and brass plaque denotes Pearson Field as an American Institute of Aeronautics and Astronautics Historic Site.

Two of its historic buildings are its single-story Airfield Office and historic hangar. The office was built in 1918 as part of the Spruce Cut-Up Plant. In 1922, it became part of airfield operations and then moved in 1929 to its new location by the museum. Refurbished in 2000, it's now

Resting before Pearson Field's historic hanger sits pilot Leah Hing's 1931 Fleet Model 7 after its return to Pearson. *John Shirron.*

A National Park Service park ranger tells Pearson's history from its aviation camp, military airfield and Spruce Mill days up through World War II. *Fort Vancouver National Historic Site.*

meeting and office space for the National Park Service. The 1921 hangar is in the National Register of Historic Places. Around 1924, the Army Air Service moved it to its current location. Today, it provides an excellent venue for weddings, luncheons, parties, celebrations of life and other large events. Its barn-style doors bring the indoors of the hangar to the outdoors for special events.

Although neglected by aviation historians, Pearson Airpark's roots run more than a century deep in the story of flight. Its contributions include much forgotten or ignored by historians generally focusing on broad swaths of the aviation narrative. Yet Pearson's roots cling to many stories, ranging from a dirigible delivery of letters, aerobatic feats, airmail origins, the start of airlines, the beginnings of the Air Corps, the training of early women pilots and the courage of the men and women risking their lives to extend the boundaries of aviation.

For historians interested in Soviet aviation, the Fort Vancouver National Park Service provides some research materials found nowhere else. The museum's collection keeps expanding thanks to dedicated volunteers who re-created a Curtiss Pusher, the acquisition of Leah Hing's plane and donors of manuscripts and artifacts. Both add to the significance of the field and museum. After more than a century, Pearson Field remains not only an operational airport but also one of the few airfields left with a prewar ambiance and persists among the oldest airfields in continuous use, making it a unique place in time.

Appendix A

FULL- AND PART-TIME PACIFIC AIR TRANSPORT PILOTS (NORTHERN ROUTE)

THE NORTHERN AIRMAIL ROUTE included Pearson Field beginning in 1926 and ended sometime after 1927 when Portland's Swan Island officially opened.

1. Frank Anderline
2. Vernon "Vern" Bookwalter
3. Ray Bouderaux**
4. Lonnie Brennan
5. Russ Cunningham*
6. Grant Donaldson*
7. C.H. Dunbar
8. Al Gilhousen*
9. John Gugliemetti
10. Jess Hart
11. Joe Johnson
12. Hershel Laughlin
13. Heber Miller*
14. R.B. Patterson**
15. Ray Small
16. Joe Smith
17. Charles B. Stead
18. Grover Tyler*

*Retired with United Airlines
**Died in mail crash
Source: Ron Bartley, *Vern Worst and the Pacific Air Transport Air Mail* (Interactive Media Publishing, 2006), 61.

Appendix B

PEARSON 1925 DEDICATION EVENTS AND WINNERS (WHERE KNOWN)

Event	Result
Landing on mark (landing closest to the center of a circle)	1st. Lieutenant John Griffith (Kelly Field) 2nd. Sergeant Kelly (Crissy Field) 3rd. Lieutenant De Garmo (Eugene Forest Patrol)
Curtiss JN (Jenny) speed race (2 laps around 3 pylons)	1st. Lieutenant A.B. McKenzie (Pearson Field) 2nd. Captain J.R Cunningham (Pearson Field) 3rd. Lieutenant H. Walker (Sand Point)
DH (De Havilland) speed race (3 laps around 3 pylons)	1st. Lieutenant C.V. Haynes (Crissy Field) 2nd. Captain Lowell Smith (Pearson Field). Smith was a member of the Army's 1924 Around the World tour. 3rd. Lieutenant Oakley G. Kelly (Pearson Field)

Event	Result
Competitive formation (Curtiss) (judged on assembly time and number of planes)	1st. Sand Point Field 2nd. Pearson Field 3rd. Spokane Field
Competition formation (De Havilland) (judged on assembly time and number of planes)	1st. Crissy Field 2nd. Kelly Field 3rd. Eugene Forest Patrol
Curtiss JN relay race (competitors fly and land 3 planes in succession)	
Stunt flying	Archie Roth Adrian Van Aeist N.B. Evans
Open handicap speed race (3 laps, 3 pylons)	
National Guard speed race (2 laps, 3 pylons)	
Commercial plane speed race (2 laps, 3 pylons)	
Parachute jump (altitude and landing accuracy)	Private Alca Button Sergeant Henry Kruger
Bomb dropping (altitude 1,000 feet, drop "bomb" for accuracy)	Lieutenant Taylor and Lieutenant Hayes (Crissy Field)
Aerial combat	Demonstration
Wing walking	Demonstration

Source: Walker.

Appendix C

PEARSON AIRPARK CHRONOLOGY

1825	Hudson's Bay Company dedicates Fort Vancouver on the north bank of the Columbia River.
1849	Army establishes Vancouver Barracks. Fort Vancouver jointly occupied by U.S. Army and the British until 1860, as the HBC transitions Fort Vancouver to British Columbia.
1905	The field's first aviation use. Lincoln Beachy pilots the City of Portland dirigible from the 1905 Lewis & Clark Exposition, landing at the Vancouver Barracks polo field near today's O.O. Howard House.
1910	A newspaper article mentions the "aviation camp" at Vancouver Barracks, establishing its long history in aviation.
1911	Charles Walsh becomes the first to fly over Vancouver, Washington.
1912	Christofferson conducts the first Northwest heavier-than-air passenger flight from Vancouver, taking Edna Becker, his future wife, aloft. Christofferson flies off the top of Portland's Multnomah Hotel, landing at the Vancouver Barracks polo field. An exhibition by Walter Edwards flies the first airmail between Oregon and Washington, landing at Pearson Field.

1917–1918	World War I: the Spruce Cut-Up Mill dominates the polo field, contributing to aviation production until November 1918. Only flights are for scouting forest fires.
1920s	The Army Air Corps develops the airfield, and landing areas are improved for airplanes. Surplus Curtiss JN-4 aircraft, also known as "Jennies," are first sold in 1920.
1921	The U.S. Air Service and forest patrols use Pearson Airfield, but occasional flooding leads to discontinuation of operations.
1921–1923	Military airfield established; Lieutenant Laurence Barrett Hickham, commander.
1923–1924	Lieutenant James F. Powell, commander.
1924	The 321st Observation Squadron arrives at Pearson Field under Lieutenant Oakley Kelly. Vern Bookwalter pilots the Ku Klux Klan "flaming cross" flight over county fairgrounds. Lieutenant Colonel Jason M. Walling, acting commander. Army's around-the-world Douglas Cruisers land at Pearson Field escorted by Lieutenant Oakley Kelly. They land a second time on their return.
Mid-1920s	First commercial flights started.
1924–1926	Tex Rankin Flight School operates for about eighteen months. Following Army orders, all JN-4s are destroyed at Pearson Field.
1924–1928	Lieutenant Oakley Kelly, commander.

1925	Pearson Field dedicated, becoming the name given to the western portion of the field. An Army Air Corps directive prohibits civilian use, resulting in the formation of an eastern landing area. While railroad held the eastern end, Army owned the western end designated as Pearson Airpark.
1926	First U.S. Post Office sanctioned interstate airmail by Pacific Air Transport.
1927	Charles Lindbergh flies under the Bridge of the Gods (Cascade Locks, Oregon) and later drops a message at Pearson Field collected by the American Legion. The message has since disappeared. He visited Wally Olson at Evergreen Field later at an unknown date.
1928–1929	Lieutenant Aubrey I. Eagle, commander.
1929	First Russian landing. Louis Proctor Air Jubilee.
1929–1933	Lieutenant Carlton Foster Bond (first tour)
1930	The City of Vancouver leases the eastern half of the airfield, dedicating it as Vancouver Municipal Airport.
1933–1939	Lieutenant Paul Burrows, commander. Second Russian landing, 1937.
1939–1942	Captain Carlton Foster Bond, commander (second tour).
1940s	The city obtains a long-term lease for the eastern landing area, later purchased in 1972.
1941	The U.S. Army ceases use of Pearson Airpark. Western half unused due to Columbia River flooding.
1941–1942	Captain J.P. Cox, commander.
1941–1943	Captain Harry L. Cole, commander.
1943–1946	Two hundred Italian cobelligerents use Pearson hangar, Camp Hathaway and Vancouver Barracks.

1944–1945	U.S. government plans a Pearson Airpark conversion and completes grading streets and naming them but abandons the work.
1946	After World War II, the Army declares Pearson surplus property in 1946. But prior to the Army's acquisition, the 1925 fence separating the western and eastern runways is removed in the middle of the night. The Pearson Airpark name is now used for the single runway of part grass and part gravel.
1949	The City of Vancouver acquires Pearson Airpark, including aviation support buildings, from the War Assets Administration.
1950s	The finances of the airport and its future are shaky. Much discussion about the future of Pearson Airpark; nothing significant happens.
1959	The City of Vancouver sells part of Pearson Field and disbands the Vancouver Board of Aeronautics.
1960s	Serious discussion around Pearson's existence. Many proposals. Nothing happens, setting stage for change in 1971.
1961	The city concludes sale of a portion of Pearson to Washington Department of Transportation.
1963	First July Fourth fireworks begin at Pearson Airpark, grows into the largest fireworks display west of the Mississippi.
1964	City acquires 4.7 acres of surplus land from government and uses it to extend the runway from 3,400 feet to 4,200 feet, adding 800 feet as an overrun.
1966	Pearson east and west runways are paved, but the 800-foot overrun is left as grass. (This might have been the first FAA grant for Pearson Airpark.)

1970s	First new commercial buildings, numbers 101 and 105. Building 105 is built by the Bonneville Power Administration. While an exact date is not known, photos from the early 1970s show the buildings at their current locations.
1971	Negotiations with NPS begin to purchase the western part of Pearson Field, with the stipulations of funding for airport relocation, removing the upper landing for Fort Vancouver and allowing the city to use the airport. Sale proceeds are spent according to City of Vancouver Resolution M-1521. Pearson benefactor Melvin "Jack" Murdock crashes into the Columbia River and dies.
1972	Vancouver sells 72.57 acres west to NPS for $544,500, with funds for airport relocation and railroad land purchase. New thirty-year Military Operation Area (MOA) lease allows $1 per year use. Pearson is scheduled to close in 2002. Burlington Northern sells 61.8 acres for $463,500.
1975	Serious plans are made to site a new airport called the Pioneer site at Ridgefield. Later, the plan is abandoned.
1980s	Two new hangars, A and B, are built on land purchased from the railroad, likely added after the Pioneer airport was not built. Both remain in use. Sometime in the 1980s, the Pearson Airpark Historical Society formed; exact date is unknown.
1982	New 30-foot-wide taxiway added to Pearson, a major improvement to an Airport Layout Plan created, approved and funded by the FAA.
1985	First mention of Pearson Field Historical Society as a nonprofit collecting funds from member dues, admission fees, grants, donations and money from the City of Vancouver.

1987	Vancouver's leaders decide to keep Pearson open beyond 2002, allowing its continued operation and the establishment of a museum. Pearson Historical Society activates. Fiftieth anniversary of Russian transpolar flight.
1989	President George H.W. Bush signs a transportation bill extending the airport's closure until 2009, requiring the FAA to fund it, removing the 2002 closure.
1990	The Vancouver Historical Study Commission is established to study the historic, cultural, natural and recreational significance. Pearson's future is debated, as is the need for congressional action. The Pearson Aviation Historical Society (PAHS) provides the first systematic collection of materials relevant to Pearson's history. Registration application is submitted to National Register of Historic Places.
1991	Leah Hing is reunited with her Fleet 7 during an antique air show at Evergreen Field.
1992	Tom Murphy replicates the first airmail flight between Oregon and Washington.
1993	In April 1993, the Vancouver Historical Study Commission publishes a feasibility study for the creation of the National Historic Reserve, including Pearson.
1994	Pearson Airpark will not close in 2002, as per a 1994 Memorandum of Agreement between NPS and City of Vancouver. The agreement continues the use and development of the airpark and museum area. T-hangars and non-historic buildings are to be moved by 2003.
1995	Tom Murphy replicates Silas Christofferson's flight off the Multnomah Hotel.

1996	A federal law extends Pearson Field's life until 2022, and the Vancouver National Historic Reserve is established. Public Law 104–333 establishes Vancouver National Historic Reserve. It does not include city land located in the northeast corner outside of the East Gate.
1996–1997	Eight hangers with sixteen T-hangers are built on city-owned property. Bonds are issued, to be paid off in 2018 from airport funds.
2000s	Sometime in the early 2000s, the Pearson Airpark Historical Society dissolved, exact date unknown.
2005	Last mention of Pearson Field Historical Society in local press.
2007	Vancouver National Historic Reserve partnership forms with National Park Service, U.S. Army, the State of Washington and the City of Vancouver.
2010	New land use protections by state law discourage incompatible uses near Pearson Field.
2011	New forty-year lease for 20.5 acres from National Park Service. Expires 2051.
2012	Receives national recognition through the American Institute of Aeronautics and Astronautics (AIAA) as a historic aerospace site.
2013	National Park Service begins to directly staff the museum. Pearson Field Education Center is established and operates out of the western hangar on the north side of the field.
2014	Pearson budget goes from red to black due to the elimination of the 12.84 percent Washington State Leasehold Tax (LHT). The city receives over $400,000 from the State of Washington, depositing funds in the Airport Enterprise Fund.
2017	Height restrictions on buildings are placed in the airport's flight path to protect Pearson Field's future.

2018	All bonds for new hangars are paid off. Pearson Field is debt free. Volunteer-built Curtiss Pusher replica is completed.
2020	The City of Vancouver National Park Service director sends a report to the NPS director as required by the 1994 Military Operation Area (MOA), highlighting the collaborative efforts to support Pearson Field's continued operation and its historic value.
2022	Leah Hing's Fleet 7 returns to Pearson Museum. It is currently on display.
2025	One hundredth anniversary of Pearson Field military dedication and naming. Three World War I mortars are found and defused by law enforcement. Trump administration cuts National Park Service Staff.
2030	One hundredth anniversary of the opening of Vancouver Municipal Field.

BIBLIOGRAPHY

Archives

Clark County Historical Museum
Eisenhower Archives, Jacqueline Cochran folders
Fort Vancouver National Historic Site
National Archives
Oregon Aviation Historical Society
Oregon Historical Society

Books

Arbon, Lee. *They Also Flew: The Enlisted Pilot Legacy—1912–1942*. Smithsonian Institution Press, 1992.

Bartley, Ron. *Vern Gorst and the Pacific Air Transport Air Mail*. Interactive Media Publishing, 2006.

Bohrer, Walt. *America's Famous Fliers—A Pictorial History: Tex Rankin*. Watsonville Press, 1966.

———. *Black Cats and Outside Loops: Tex Rankin, Pilot and Legend*. Piere Publishers, 1989.

Bohrer, Walt, and Ann Bohrer. *Twenty Smiling Eagles*. Vantage Press, 1962.

Glines, Carroll, V. *The First Round-the-World Flight: Around the World in 175 Days*. Smithsonian Institution Press, 2001.

Gorst, Wilber H. *Pioneer and Granddad of United Air Lines*. Gorst Publications, 1979.

Grove, Tim. *First Flight Around the World: The Adventures of American Fliers Who Won the Race*. National Air and Space Museum, 2015.

Holmes, Donald B. *Air Mail: An Illustrated History, 1793–1981*. Clarkson N. Potter Publishers, 1981.

Lucia, Ellis. *The Big Blow: The Story of the Pacific Northwest's Columbus Day Storm*. Overland West Press, 1967.

Marrero, Frank. *Lincoln Beachey: The Man Who Owned the Sky*. Scottwell Associates, 1997.

Maurer, Maurer. *General Histories: Aviation in the U.S. Army 1919–1939*. United States Air Force History Research Center, Office of Air Force History, United States Air Force, 1987.

Moolman, Valerie. *The Road to Kitty Hawk*. Time-Life Books, 1980.

Richards, Leverett G. *Elephants Don't Snore*. Rose Wind Press, 1996.

Simons, David, and Thomas Wirthington. *The History of Flight*. Paragon Publishing, 2004.

Time-Life Book Series on Aviation

Walker, Jon. *A Century Airborne: Air Trails of Pearson Airpark*. Rose Wind, 1994.

DVDs and Videos

A&E Television (History). *First Flight Around the World*. 2005.

"Flight of Fancy: A Reenactment of the Daring 1912 Flight from the Roof of Portland, Oregon's Multnomah Hotel." Pacific Vista Publishing, LLC, Portland, OR, 2002.

"I Remember Pearson Field." Pacific Vista Publishing, LLC, Portland, OR, 2008.

Taylor, Heather A. (director and writer). *Breaking Through the Clouds: The First Women's National Air Derby*, 2010.

YouTube. "Additional Footage from Pearson Field." https://www.youtube.com/watch?v=0VqqR_Olx0I.

———. "Flight Enthusiasts Talk About Pearson Field Videos." http://couv.com/programs/originals/pearson-field-airport.

———. "Flying into Pearson Field (VUO) Special Flight Rules Area (SFRA)." https://www.youtube.com/watch?v=XXQV1Amae4A.

———. "Pearson Field Airport—Vancouver, WA." https://www.youtube.com/watch?v=X2pMirqKghs.

———. "Pearson Field Trailer." https://www.youtube.com/watch?v=RSfx6wlM4G0.

———. "What's New at Pearson Air Museum?" https://www.youtube.com/watch?v=1ZhCcMM0xGo.

———. "WWI Lumber Mill at Pearson/Fort Vancouver." https://www.youtube.com/watch?v=d_wSUiiPrOU.

Journals, Magazines, Publications

AOPA Pilot
The California Highway Patrolman
Clark County History
Flying Magazine
Forest History Today
Oregon Aviation Museum Newsletter
Oregon Historical Quarterly
Oregon Pilots' Association Newsletter
Radio Control Modeler
Reason
Smithsonian Magazine

Newspapers

Arlington Times
The Brainerd Daily Dispatch
The Capital-Journal (Salem, OR)
Centralia Daily Chronicle-Examiner
The Columbian
Corvallis Gazette-Times
Evening World Herald Omaha
Klamath News
Lafayette (IN) Journal and Courier
The Lincoln Star
Los Angeles Times
The News-Herald
New York Times
Norfolk Weekly News Journal
The Olympian
Omaha Sunday Bee
Oregon Daily Journal
The Oregonian
Oregon Journal
Oregon Statesman
Popular Aviation
Portsmouth Daily Times
The Republic (Columbus, IN)
San Diego Union
San Francisco Examiner
Spokane Chronicle
The Spokesman Review
Star Tribune
The Tacoma Daily Ledger
The Tacoma News Tribune
Times Colonist (Victoria, BC)
Trenton Evening Times
Tualatin Times
Vancouver Columbian
Vancouver Weekly Columbian
The World (Coos Bay, OR)

Reports

American Institute of Aeronautics and Astronautics Historic Aerospace Site: Pearson Field. Vancouver, WA, 2012.

Hardesty, Von (PhD). *Historical Overview of Pearson Airfield*. 1992. https://npshistory.com/publications/fova/pearson-airfield.pdf.

Sinclair, Donna L. *Part II, The Waking of a Military Town: Vancouver, Washington and the Vancouver National Historic Reserve, 1898-1920, with Suggestions for Further Research*. Fort Vancouver National Historic Site, January 2005.

———. *Part III, Riptide on the Columbia: A Military Community Between the Wars, Vancouver, Washington and the Vancouver National Historic Reserve, 1920–1942, with Suggestions for Further Research*. Fort Vancouver National Historic Site, 2005.

Stearns, Cuthbert P. *History of Spruce Production Division and United States Spruce Production Corporation*. Portland, OR: Kilham Stationery & Printing Co., c. 1920.

Tonsfeldt, Ward, PhD. *Spruce Trail Guide: The U.S. Army Spruce Production Division Mill*. (brochure) Cultural Fort Vancouver National Historic Site, September 2010.

———. *The U.S. Army Spruce Production Division at Vancouver Barracks, Washington, 1917–1919*. (Prepared for Fort Vancouver National Historic Site, National Park Service). March 1, 2013.

Websites

Fort Vancouver National Historic Site | www.nps.gov/fova/index.htm
HistoryNet | https://www.historynet.com
Wikipedia | https://www.wikipedia.org

For a complete bibliography contact the author at clarkcohist@gmail.com.

INDEX

Y

Z

ABOUT THE AUTHOR

A freelance writer in Vancouver, Washington, Martin Middlewood earned a graduate degree in writing and completed graduate studies in American history at Eastern Washington University. As a writer and ghostwriter, he's written about medicine, technology, AI, construction and the environment. He edits *Clark County History* and writes a local history column for *The Columbian*. In 2017, the Clark County Historical Society presented him with the W. Foster Hidden Award.